T0248505

THE COCKTAIL CABINET

THE COCKTAIL CABINET

The art, science and
pleasure of mixing
the perfect drink

ZOE BURGESS

MITCHELL
BEAZLEY

First published in Great Britain
in 2022 by Mitchell Beazley,
an imprint of
Octopus Publishing Group Ltd
Carmelite House
50 Victoria Embankment
London EC4Y 0DZ
www.octopusbooks.co.uk

An Hachette UK Company
www.hachette.co.uk

Distributed in the US by
Hachette Book Group
1290 Avenue of the Americas
4th and 5th Floors
New York, NY 10104

Distributed in Canada by
Canadian Manda Group
664 Annette St.
Toronto, Ontario, Canada
M6S 2C8

ISBN 978-1-78472-799-4

A CIP catalogue record for this
book is available from the British
Library.

Printed and bound in China

10 9 8 7 6 5 4 3 2 1

Group Publisher Denise Bates
Senior Editor Alex Stetter
Art Director Jaz Bahra
Copy Editor Joanna Smith
Photographer Andre Ainsworth
Props Stylist Luis Peral
Drinks Stylist Lola Faura
Illustrator Diana Hlevnjak
Senior Production Controller
  Allison Gonsalves

Thank you to every person I worked or collaborated with. Each of you taught me something about the craft of flavour and the art of communication. Without you, this book wouldn't exist.

CONTENTS

INTRODUCTION

Flavour excites me. It's such a personal experience that is difficult to quantify, yet something we love to share and communicate with others.

I think about flavour all the time: 'How can what I eat or drink satisfy me on an emotional level and how can I share that with others?' While it's important to me to put good-quality products into my body, what I really care about is satisfying my soul. For a long time I took that desire at face value; I consumed food and drink without thinking about why I and others were enjoying it. Then I had my first well-made, considered cocktail – an Aviation containing gin, maraschino liqueur and lemon juice – and it blew my mind. I left that experience asking myself, 'How did that single small vessel, containing one complete liquid, make me feel like I'd had the most personal flavour experience?' It was as if I'd just witnessed a magic trick. I was desperate to uncover the secrets.

In a sense, it's hard to think of a cocktail as being personal – a Martini in one bar can look the same as any other. But looks are deceiving and not all Martinis taste the same; that's the magic behind cocktails. They are the ultimate vessels for flavour personalization and the creation of a shared moment between host and guest.

After my revelation, I knew that if I could gain an understanding of how the ingredients in a cocktail interact with each other, I'd have endless opportunities for enjoyable flavour experiences. I knew I could explore my personal tastes and why they existed. And through the act of hosting guests, I could share my tastes with others in an enjoyable way. And so my journey started.

Through this book I will share with you what I discovered and my personal approach to cocktail making at home, which is led by simplicity and balance. I won't be focusing on the history of certain cocktails and the most 'authentic' recipes, but their structure and flavour profiles, breaking them down into building blocks so that you can understand how an ingredient works and why a finished cocktail tastes so good. I am a firm believer in building solid foundations and hope this method will allow you to move in whichever direction suits you. This book will set you on your own path of discovery, using your personal preference to decide which cocktails to try next. It will teach you how to make best use of the ingredients you have to hand and, ultimately, help you to create valued and shared rituals at home, concentrating on the quality and experience of the drinks you make more than the alcohol they contain.

HOW TO USE THIS BOOK

To make the world of cocktails more approachable, I have split this book into two sections. The first covers the practical elements involved in making drinks – think of it as an instruction manual with advice to help simplify the preparation of drinks. You will find details about the equipment required, the best way to set up a bar at home and definitions of common cocktail-making terms. This section also covers the techniques involved in making cocktails (and where appropriate the reasons behind them) so that when it comes to the recipes in Section Two I can focus on the structure and flavour of the drinks.

I've included a lot of information about ingredients in Section One, but by no means do you need all of these things. My goal is to make cocktails at home efficient, and that includes the price. The last thing I want you to do is feel like you need to purchase every item on the list; you do not. My suggestion is first to digest some of the information in this book, learn about your preferences and find a focused place to start. The pay-off will be that all purchases are considered for their flavour profile and versatility within and across the cocktail categories, so hopefully you'll need to invest in fewer products.

A significant part of Section One delves into basic tastes, overall flavour and the principles of cocktail structure. I'll explain the details you need to better understand your preferences and ultimately to help you make cocktails to suit your tastes and needs.

Section Two applies all of the information you will have learned to specific cocktail categories and the drinks within them. A note on this: there are many ways to categorize cocktails. I have chosen a way that I feel most suits this book and will help you learn and connect all of the dots.

As this book is about flavour as much as cocktails, it's important to me to be efficient with ingredients. The final chapter introduces some bespoke recipes to inspire you to evolve your cocktails at home. This involves looking at the ingredients in your kitchen cupboard and working with them as flavour substitutions within a recipe. My hope is that, once you've understood the building blocks of a cocktail, you can create cocktails to suit you from the ingredients you have to hand.

A NOTE ON MEASUREMENTS

All the cocktails in this book were created and tested using metric measurements. I use a set of metric measuring spoons (see page 25) and to achieve the best results, I suggest you do the same. If you prefer to work in ounces, measurements that reflect my original metric measurements as accurately as possible have also been provided.

FLAVOUR PROFILES

On pages 42–53, I introduce some basic ingredients – a selection of spirits, from vodka to absinthe, suitable for use across many different types of cocktail. Each brief flavour profile is accompanied by an illustration that offers a visual snapshot of the aroma, taste, texture and impact of a particular spirit from my personal point of view – the closest we can get to a tutored tasting session in the pages of a book.

RECIPE ILLUSTRATIONS

Each cocktail recipe is accompanied by an illustration showing the composition of the drink – the proportions of the liquid ingredients, any ice or garnishes and the type of glass used. The key colours used in the ingredient flavour profiles also appear in these illustrations, to give you a feel for the overall flavour of the drink.

DIRTY GIN MARTINI

 GIN

 DRY VERMOUTH

 OLIVE BRINE

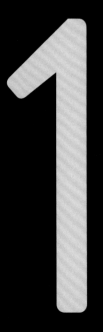

1

THE PRINCIPLES

CHAPTER 1:
HOW TO APPROACH
COCKTAIL MAKING

The cocktails we know today have been shaped by many factors, including history, the style of the bartenders who have made them, the flavour preferences of the customers drinking them and the quality of ingredients used. As recipes have evolved over time, we are left not only with a great selection of different styles of cocktails to explore but in some cases several versions of each of these drinks. This wealth of knowledge is a great tool, but it can make approaching cocktails quite daunting – you don't want to choose a drink and not like it, or invest in expensive products when you don't know what to expect from the end results. If you want to create delicious cocktails at home, how do you know where to start? The answer is by learning about the basic structure of classic cocktails and identifying your basic taste and overall flavour preferences.

What exactly is structure in the context of cocktails? It is the arrangement and relationship between a drink's ingredients. A well-structured cocktail tastes balanced; this means that the sensation of alcohol along with the basic tastes of sweet, sour, bitter and in some cases salt and umami are all in proportion to each other. That's not to say that they should all taste equally as strong as each other, but that the sum of their parts creates a harmonious experience. Aromatic profiles feed into this base structure, contributing to an overall pleasing flavour.

When creating cocktails, I'm driven by detail. I like to understand the flavour of the ingredients so that I can combine them to create a new experience for myself and others. However, my approach always takes into account the structure of the particular classic cocktail I'm working with. I know that a syrup needs to be of a certain sweetness in order to work with the other ingredients in the cocktail. If that syrup contains a fruit that will add acid to the drink, I will also need to take that into account. The fruit I've used will have a specific aromatic profile, so I will need to ensure that works with the aromatic profile of the spirit used in the drink. It is a case of paying attention to the effects of an ingredient – as one changes, it affects how the other ingredients work together.

Having an understanding of the ingredients and how they work together means that I can choose better-suited ingredients or methods of making, while ensuring that the end result is still a balanced drink. I appreciate my goal here is to break down structure in a basic way and at the moment it does not sound very basic. But it's this level of detail that sets a great drink apart from the rest, and it's why classic cocktails become classics – their structure is referenced over and over again, as their balance works so well.

It's important to realize that the great thing about structure is, well, its structure – it can be understood and learned. Ultimately, when you start to understand the structure of cocktails, you can identify the basic tastes and aromatic building blocks within a mixed drink. This information becomes a guide that will work hand in hand with your personal preferences.

When we come to the cocktail recipes later in the book, the links between the structure of the drinks within each category will become more apparent. But right now I need to give you a foundation to start building on, so I've broken down some key thoughts and considerations to understand and explore.

TASTE AND FLAVOUR ARE DIFFERENT THINGS

The words 'taste' and 'flavour' have become interchangeable in common usage, but technically they are two different things.

'Taste' refers to our experience of the basic tastes – sweet, sour, bitter, salt and umami – and is experienced through the taste buds on our tongues and in our mouths. The word 'tastant' refers to a chemical that stimulates one of our basic tastes via our taste buds.

'Flavour', on the other hand, refers to the whole experience of a food or liquid we consume. This includes its appearance, aromatic profile, taste, texture and any chemesthetic sensations such as hot and cold, the burning sensation from ingredients such as chilli or the cooling sensation from mint.

TASTE GIVES US A FOUNDATION TO WORK FROM

The relationship of the five basic tastes is important, as it builds the first layer within the structure of a cocktail. You may be working with the most wonderful aromatic ingredients, but if one tastant is too strong or weak, a cocktail can become undrinkable and no addition or change in aromatics will hide the imbalance. So it's important to pay attention to the basic tastes within your cocktail. If you need to make a change or substitute an ingredient, think about the consequence of that change. Look out for any further adjustments you may need to make in order to keep the overall taste balanced.

At some point you may want to adjust the balance of your cocktails to suit your taste preference. A common example of this is sweetness: some people like a sweeter drink, while others will prefer it with less sugar. You'll notice that, where appropriate, the recipes in the book contain guidance on what to take into account when you make an ingredient swap or adjust the quantity of an ingredient. Generally speaking, always start with a single adjustment so that you can fully understand how that one change affects the whole cocktail. You can then build up or down from there, moving on to a second change if desired. The Old Fashioned recipes on pages 124 and 126 are good examples of how this works with sugar and sweetness levels.

FLAVOUR EXPANDS OUR FOUNDATIONS

When it comes to food and drink, our choices are often driven by the aromas we want to experience. You'll notice that some cocktail recipes are exactly the same apart from using a different spirit. Compare the Whiskey Sour on page 171 which uses Bourbon with the Scotch Whisky Sour on page 175 to appreciate how a different spirit can affect flavour – the basic recipe and therefore the taste structure is the same, but the overall flavour is different.

In some cases, swapping a spirit to achieve a different flavour can have further-ranging consequences and a second ingredient in the cocktail needs to change to maintain balance. To appreciate this, we can see what happens when we swap the gin for vodka in a Martini recipe. As vodka has less of an aromatic profile than gin, we need to reduce the amount of vermouth, our other highly aromatized ingredient, in order to create a flavour-balanced cocktail. Yes, the experience will be different, as vermouth adds a touch of sweetness and bitterness to a Martini and we have now reduced these tastants – the drink will be drier and punchier in the sensation of alcohol on the palate. But it will still be balanced in flavour and your motivation for making a Vodka Martini (see pages 112–113) rather than a Gin Martini (see pages 104–107) will be your personal preference.

PREFERENCE IS VITAL

Everything I taste, even the things I don't like, teaches me something about my preferences and contributes to my instinct for flavour. The best way to learn about your preference is to look at the choices you make when it comes to cocktails. Do you naturally gravitate towards a certain style of drink or ingredient? Sometimes I find it easier to turn this around and think about what I don't enjoy or want to taste; I then look at what options I have left after I've ruled out the things I dislike.

The next step in understanding your preference is to taste a cocktail you like and really think about what it is that you are experiencing. Ask yourself why you enjoy it and explore this in more detail. Let's take sour as an example – perhaps your motivation for choosing a sour cocktail is simply because you like its acidic taste, or perhaps it is because the acidity is cutting through the sweetness? In other words, you may realize you don't like sweet drinks. This is enlightening because it means your taste preference is sour, because it offers a less sweet-tasting drink. As a new experience, you may next like to try a savoury cocktail, as these are also less sweet in taste.

Aroma-wise, perhaps you like sour cocktails because the citrus used in these drinks adds a clean, bright and fresh note? Is it the clean coolness of these aromas that you appreciate, and as a contrast, how does that make you feel about heavier woody notes? Do these aromas have a positive association from a past experience? Take note of how you feel and use this information as guidance on where to start on your cocktail journey with this book.

STRUCTURE IS NOT NECESSARILY RIGID OR FIXED

After what we have just discussed, this perhaps sounds like a contradiction. But while you learn a little more about structure, you will also be learning about the capabilities of ingredients and cocktails. Ultimately, this knowledge will help you to identify 'gaps' in structure or 'bridges' you can build so that you can explore different ingredients or flavour additions in a drink. This is how modern-day cocktails are created; we identify the gaps in the classics and use personal preferences and a change in the ingredients or technique to push the structure of a cocktail Winto something exciting and new to experience.

CHAPTER 2:
THE SET-UP

One of the most incredible things to observe in a cocktail bar is the bartenders at work. I say bartenders because, if you're in a great venue, you'll notice that every member of the team behind the bar and on the floor is on exactly the same wavelength. It's as if they are all taking part in the same dance. Making drinks in a working bar is a very physical and pressured experience, so reducing the process down to as few exact moves as possible means the team can achieve a flow of service that they all intrinsically understand. Members of the team will assist each other to ease the physical rigours and of course ensure drinks are served perfectly and quickly. Though making cocktails at home is less pressured, there are some great lessons we can learn from the bar environment. Our starting point is the bar station; get this set-up right and making drinks at home will be much simpler and more fun.

The bar station is a dedicated space to accommodate all of your cocktail-making equipment and ingredients. This space should be set up in a practical, user-friendly way. In the same way a modern kitchen is designed to take into account the spatial relationship between fridge/freezer, sink and cooker, a bar station should ideally be set up with a spatial relationship between fridge/freezer, sink and work surface. This means that the kitchen is really the best place for a bar station. I know this might mean you, as host, are taken away from the party, but if you can get your bar station set up correctly, you will be making drinks quickly and be released from the kitchen – in a worst-case scenario, I hope the party comes to you!

Start by choosing a work surface that can handle spilt liquids without damage and is well positioned between your sink and fridge/freezer. Don't underestimate the need for a sink when making cocktails. You'll need running water to clean your hands and cocktail-making equipment, as well as a sink to throw used ice away. Having access to a fridge/freezer is handy, as it means you can keep Champagne and mixers cool, which will improve the quality of your drinks. It also allows you to keep glasses in the freezer, which elevates the whole drinking experience for those cocktails requiring a chilled glass. If you have space in the freezer to do this, you won't regret it. If not, you can use ice to chill your glasses, which we'll discuss in the next chapter. Don't forget to have a bin tucked away yet easily accessible; rubbish can then be dealt with straight away, saving you a lot of time and helping your bar station stay clear and clean.

A note on hygiene: you are serving liquids that will be consumed, so please be food safe. Clean your work surface appropriately before you start and ensure all equipment is clean and safe to use with no chipped glassware. Keep a cleaning cloth to hand to quickly wipe up any spillages when making drinks and avoid a sticky bar station. Keep your hands clean, with tea towels to hand to keep them dry during the cocktail-making process. When you finish making and serving a cocktail, you will need to discard the used ice from your cocktail shaker, tin or mixing glass in a sink and rinse out the vessel with clean running water. Any strainers and bar spoons will need to be rinsed too. This removes any leftover ingredients and flavours, setting the equipment up ready to make the next round of drinks. For the very same reason, measuring spoons and jiggers can be kept in a bowl filled with cold water. Once used, you can drop the spoon or jigger back into the bowl and it will sufficiently rinse itself. If you are making a lot of drinks, I recommend you change the water in the bowl a few times during the session.

Just like with cooking, preparation is key when making cocktails. Having all your ingredients to hand and your cocktail recipes visible will speed up the process of making drinks. If you are hosting a number of people and plan on making a cocktail that requires fresh citrus juice, I suggest you pre-squeeze your juice a few hours in advance and keep it in the fridge until needed. You can also pass your juice through a sieve or fine strainer in advance, to remove the bits from the liquid. A tip to maximize the use of your citrus fruit: if you need citrus-peel garnishes, cut them from your fruit first, then juice the fruit. Citrus garnishes can again be prepped a few hours in advance; keep them in a small dish in the fridge with a little damp kitchen paper on top to keep them fresh. For the best results, always use up freshly squeezed citrus juices and garnishes on the day of preparation to keep their flavours and aromas bright and avoid oxidized tastes.

THE IDEAL BAR STATION

The illustration below will help you to visualize and organize your bar station from a practical point of view in order to reduce the movement required for making drinks. Use this as a guide and take into account your available space or constraints. If you are left-handed, you may wish to reverse the arrangement.

- Aim to minimize the process of making cocktails to as few physical movements as possible. In essence, you should be able to make your cocktails while standing in one spot.
- If you don't need it, don't put it in your bar station. This applies to ingredients and equipment, and will help to keep you focused, save on space and reduce clean-up time.
- Always lead with logic – group and place ingredients in an order that mirrors the order you will use them in your cocktail recipe.
- Be space aware: think about how you will access and pick up bottles and equipment. Is there a clear path for that movement? You want to avoid causing an issue and knocking over other items.
- Be consistent: apart from adjustments for individual cocktail requirements, always set up your bar station in the same way. Each time you make a cocktail, put your equipment or ingredients back in the exact same spot you took them from. Over time, you'll develop a muscle memory that will help you to make cocktails with ease and speed.

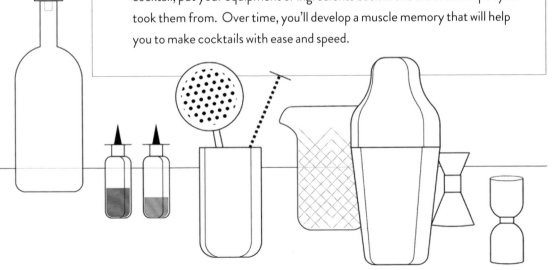

CHAPTER 3:
THE TECHNIQUES AND TERMINOLOGY OF COCKTAILS

The world of cocktails uses a language and terminology that we need to decipher. Some of these words refer to the equipment required, while others refer to the methods used to make the drinks. The goal of this chapter is, as simply as possible, to break down and define cocktail terminology. In essence, it is a detailed glossary providing information, instructions and, where appropriate, the reasons behind the methods used in mixing drinks. If you are new to cocktails, you can use the information that follows as a guide to help you decide what equipment and glassware to invest in. It is also a handy one-stop technique and terminology manual that you can refer back to when you come to make the recipes later in this book.

Where appropriate, I've provided the reasons why a piece of equipment is used or a certain technique is preferred. I hope that a few practical 'whys' will help you review your requirements, bar set-up and preferences, as well as give you an understanding of the impact of any changes you make. For example, there is no real need for you to purchase a dash bottle (see page 26) right now, especially if you are creating a cocktail-making set-up on a budget. But you should know that a dash (see page 32) from a bottle of bitters will be larger than a dash from a dash bottle, so when you do decide to purchase a beautiful dash bottle, you'll know to take this change into account and adjust your cocktail recipes accordingly.

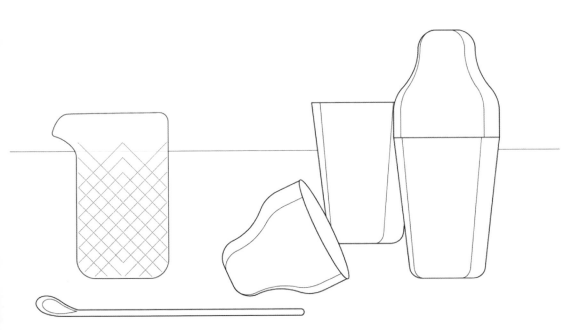

KEY EQUIPMENT

BAR KNIFE

A small, serrated knife much like a tomato knife, used to slice fruit and cut garnishes.

BAR SPOON

A teaspoon-sized spoon with a long, twisted shaft that is used to mix cocktails. The handle end of the spoon can be flat, rounded or pronged; the first two options add a little weight, which makes these spoons smoother to use. The spoon's twisted shaft helps it to glide smoothly through a liquid, and it can also be used to aid the layering of liqueurs in layered drinks.

BOSTON SHAKER

A type of cocktail shaker that traditionally has a glass half and a metal half which fit together, although shakers with two metal halves are available (often known as 'tin on tin'). By sealing the two halves together, you can shake a cocktail. You can also keep the two halves separate and stir a cocktail in either the metal or glass half –

the choice depends on the style of cocktail you are making. See also 'Cocktail tin' below and 'Mixing glass' on page 26.

COCKTAIL TIN

The metal half of a Boston or Parisian shaker, often used alone to stir a cocktail in. As metal conducts heat well, stirring in a tin is a very efficient way to cool a drink quickly, avoiding over-dilution.

FINE STRAINER

A metal strainer resembling a small fine sieve that is used to remove small ice shards from the cocktail liquid when serving. Fine strainers are sometimes referred to as 'tea strainers'.

HAWTHORNE STRAINER

A strainer used specifically for cocktails that fits snuggly into the top of a cocktail tin or mixing glass. It is used to hold the ice back in the tin or glass while you are pouring the liquid out.

JIGGER

A small metal vessel used to measure volumes of liquids accurately. Jiggers come in several sizes, and some are double-sided with a different volume at each end. I recommend having the following: 20/40ml (which will be double-sided), 25ml, 35ml and 50ml. For accurate measurements, always fill a jigger to the top or to the measurement line.

MEASURING SPOONS

Essentially baking spoons that come in a set on a ring, these are very versatile and useful in any kitchen. Normally the size of each spoon is given in millilitres as well as the teaspoon/tablespoon equivalent. Measuring spoons are vital, as they allow you to measure very small volumes of liquid accurately. To be absolutely accurate, always fill the spoon to the rim. I prefer stainless-steel sets, as they are durable and a good weight to hold and work with.

MIXING GLASS

A large and durable glass, normally with a pouring spout, that is used to stir cocktails in. A straight-walled mixing glass is most practical, as its shape makes it easier for stirring and it allows for even contact between ice and liquid, resulting in more consistent dilution and chill. Mixing glasses are used to make several classic cocktails and these glasses are often beautiful objects, which enhances the ritual and visual spectacle of cocktail making.

PARISIAN SHAKER

A cocktail shaker with a metal base, similar to a Boston shaker. The metal top used to seal this shaker has a rounded 'shoulder' shape. This is my preferred shaker, as the tin-on-tin seal is more secure than glass on tin. A Parisian shaker is normally smaller than a Boston shaker, making it easier to hold and to control the dilution of the cocktail, especially if you are making only one drink at a time. As with a Boston shaker, the base tin can be used to stir drinks in.

ADDITIONAL EQUIPMENT

DASH BOTTLE

A purpose-made small bottle used to add a dash of bitters to a drink. Dash bottles normally release less liquid than the original bottle the bitters are purchased in. If you are using a dash bottle to make the recipes in this book, you will need to increase the number of dashes by approximately 25 per cent.

ICE SCOOP

A tool used to scoop up ice and quickly fill a cocktail glass, tin or shaker.

ICE TONGS

A tool used to handle ice and place it in a drinking glass. If you do not have tongs, you can use a dessertspoon.

MEXICAN ELBOW

A manual citrus juicer that efficiently squeezes juice from citrus fruits. You can purchase a Mexican elbow that will squeeze both lemons and limes. If you have an existing citrus juicer, this should be sufficient to juice your citrus fruits.

GLASSWARE

Glassware is personal; there are so many options and beautiful pieces that you can work with, whether they are vintage or more contemporary and minimal in style. You may already have day-to-day glassware, such as wine glasses or highballs, that can be used to serve cocktails in. You may also like to invest in a few new pieces too. So that you can be efficient with cost and storage space, I have focused on the key shapes you will need for most classic cocktails and where possible suggested how a glass can double up and be used for more than one type of cocktail. To help with this, I've provided details of how the shape of the glass will affect the liquid and included the average volume for a glass style.

A note on volume: manufacturers base this measurement on the glass being full to the rim. This means the glass will normally have to be a little larger than the cocktail, as the cocktail will have a wash-line – this is the line the liquid should reach up the side of the glass and, ideally speaking, it will be somewhere between the glass rim and the width of one to two index fingers below. When selecting glassware, you will need to think about what the cocktail requires and where its wash-line will come on the glass in question.

When it comes to the cocktail recipes later in this book, I've noted an approximate volume for each diluted cocktail so that you'll have an idea of what size glassware you'll need. Your glass should be large enough to hold the liquid safel, but not so large that the glass will look empty. If your heart is set on a glass that is not quite the right volume, you can make a stylistic choice and bend the rules or look at scaling your cocktail recipe up or down to suit the glass. However, do take into account your and your guests' enjoyment of the liquid. Larger cocktails take longer to consume, so they will get warm, and for that reason I prefer smaller glasses for stronger drinks.

Finally, all of the glassware I have used for the photography in this book embraces these principles and should be commercially available, making the images a useful visual reference to help you wisely invest in and build your glassware collection over time.

COUPETTE

Also known as a saucer or coupe, this stemmed cocktail glass has a wide opening with a rounded bowl and generally holds between 100ml (3⅓oz) and 300ml (10oz) of liquid. Traditionally used for Champagne, it is sometimes criticized, as its large surface area can mean that bubbles disperse more quickly and the liquid loses its fizz over a shorter space of time. However, the large surface area also exposes the nose to more of the liquid, making any aromas easier to perceive. And if bubbles are in the mix, this effect will be amplified.

Apart from Champagne, a coupette is perfect for straight-up cocktails such as Martinis and Manhattans; as you hold this glass by its stem, heat from your hand does not transfer to the liquid. If the volume of the glass is large, it also works well for sour cocktails. This is a great versatile glass worth purchasing.

FLUTE

A stemmed glass with an average volume between 200ml (6⅔oz) and 300ml (10oz) that is traditionally used to serve Champagne. A flute has a long and lean bowl with a narrow opening. It is favoured for Champagne and Champagne cocktails, as its narrow opening holds the fizz within the glass and funnels the aroma of the drink into a concentrated area.

HIGHBALL

A stemless glass with a volume between 300ml (10oz) and 400ml (13½oz) that is used for long cocktails. Its shape is normally long and lean and suitable for holding cubed ice, which is often required for long cocktails. Ice will take up volume within a glass, so to produce consistent cocktails and avoid over-dilution, always add enough ice to fill a highball to the top of the glass. Putting less in means you increase the space for liquid, and as this style of cocktail often requires a top-up with a mixer, it will be very easy to add too much mixer, causing an over-diluted and off-balance cocktail.

If using a large highball glass, again beware of adding too much mixer. Take note of the volume of your glass and calculate the wash-line for the cocktail – it should be lower than in a smaller highball glass. To do this, follow the recipe to make a test cocktail, using a jigger to measure out the mixer. Taste your cocktail, paying attention to its overall dilution, and ensure the balance of the drink is correct. If it tastes weak, lower the planned wash-line by adding less mixer. If too strong, raise the planned wash-line by adding a touch more mixer. When it comes to mixing the drinks, you will know by eye how much mixer to add in that specific glass.

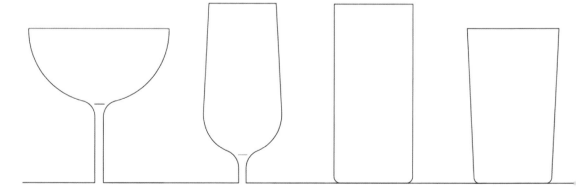

MARTINI GLASS

This stemmed glass with its classic V-shaped bowl is normally used, as its name would suggest, for serving Martinis. With a volume between 200ml (6⅔oz) and 300ml (10oz), it is also suitable for other short, straight-up and possibly sour cocktails. As with the coupette, its stem offers a place to hold the glass without adding heat to the liquid.

ROCKS GLASS

A short, wide drinking glass, sometimes referred to as a tumbler, which is suitable for short and sour cocktails. A rocks glass holds ice in any form and is usually between 250ml (8½oz) and 350ml (11⅔oz) in volume. Stylistically, this is a very versatile glass. It's not uncommon to serve a single measure of sipping spirits in a rocks glass, so our eyes have become accustomed to seeing this glass a little less full than other styles of glass.

SOURS GLASS

A sour cocktail can be served in a rocks glass or a stemmed cocktail glass such as a large coupette. It can also be served in a Nick and Nora, a goblet-shaped glass that has a volume between 150ml (5oz) and 200ml (6⅔oz). Ideally, you need a glass with a large opening so that the foam on top of the sour is just a thin layer, and when you sip the cocktail you get foam and liquid at the same time.

WINE GLASS

A stemmed glass with a classic bowl. Wine glasses come in a range of shapes and volumes depending on the style of wine they are designed to serve. There is not a set rule here for cocktails, but generally speaking, an average-sized white wine glass with a volume between 300ml (10oz) and 400ml (13½oz) is useful for larger-volume cocktails, especially if you want to mix it up a little and take

inspiration from the Spanish style of serving gin and tonic in a large balloon-shaped wine glass.

You will need to ensure your wine glass can hold enough ice to keep the drink cool as well as being able to accommodate the liquid. I recommend following the same approach described opposite for a highball glass, testing your cocktail's wash-line, balance and dilution in advance of serving drinks. Tulip wine glasses, which have more pronounced tapered sides than traditional wine glasses, have become popular for Champagne; they sit happily between a coupette and a flute, and can make very stylish glasses for Champagne cocktails.

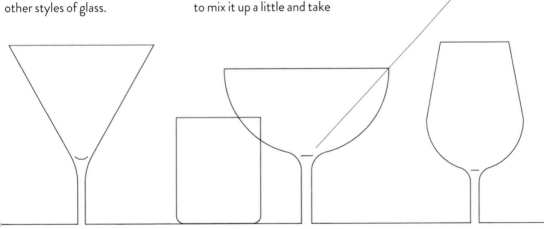

ICE AND DILUTION

Do not overlook the importance of ice – an under-diluted or over-diluted or warm cocktail is a bad drink. This one ingredient, regardless of the cocktail, can make all the difference.

Good-quality ice is solid ice; this means no dimples or hollows, as found in some cubes made in ice machines, or as small a dimple as possible. The cubes should ideally be clear, with no frost on them. The quality of ice will determine how quickly it melts or, in the case of shaken drinks, how quickly it breaks apart. This matters, as it affects the control of dilution and chilling of drinks – solid, quality ice achieves a slow and steady dilution that makes a good cocktail great. To find out more about the importance of dilution, see page 72.

Your selected cocktail recipe will specify what type of ice you need; cubed ice is most common for mixing and shaking drinks. I've listed various types of ice below, as well as defining and explaining the terms that relate to ice, temperature and dilution.

BLOCK ICE

Ice can come in specialist blocks that can be cut into large chunks. If you'd like to make more of a visual statement, blocks are great for cocktails that are served on the rocks, such as an Old Fashioned. Large blocks do require some tools and preparation to cut the ice up. You may be able to find a supplier that can cut blocks to a smaller, more usable size for you.

SHARD ICE

Essentially a long, rectangular piece of ice, great for drinks served in a highball glass. You can purchase ice in this shape or make your own by chipping pieces off a block of ice to create rougher shards.

CUBED ICE

Solid 2.5–3cm (1–1¼in) cubes of ice are used to dilute, chill and keep drinks chilled (when served over ice). Most of the recipes in this book use this style of ice. You can now purchase good-quality cubed ice from supermarkets – it's a fraction more expensive but will give you better results. If I'm hosting a group of people, I prefer to purchase ice, as it's one less thing to think about. Otherwise, I recommend the process below for making your own ice at home.

1   First boil the water you are going use to make the ice. This will help to separate the impurities, so you'll notice the resulting ice will be clear on one side with a slight cloud on the other.

2   Allow the boiled water to cool, then transfer it to an ice tray, mould or other suitable container such as a freezer-proof plastic box.

3   Place the container in the freezer and leave the water to freeze. For best results and clearer ice, allow the water to freeze slowly – this may not be something you can control in your freezer, but it's worth trying.

4   Once frozen, to keep ice fresh and free of freezer smell, store it in the freezer in a sealed bag or container.

CHILLED GLASS

Some recipes will instruct you to chill your glass before serving a cocktail in it. To do this, clear an

Milano Torino

ingredients into one liquid. As dilution lowers the alcohol content and the concentration of tastes and aromas within a drink, it will make the end cocktail flavour smoother and therefore more palatable.

ON THE ROCKS

Some recipes will instruct you to serve a cocktail over ice. The type of ice required will be specified in the cocktail recipe and depend upon on the style of drink and the glass you will be serving it in. You may be able to use several regular ice cubes, a large single cube, a sphere or chunk of ice. Large cubes and spheres can be made at home – all you'll need is the required silicone ice mould and to follow the instructions opposite for making cubed ice.

STRAIGHT UP

Some recipes will instruct you to serve a cocktail 'straight up', which means without any ice.

appropriate space in your freezer and place your glasses in there – they will take an hour or so to chill down. If you don't have enough space in your freezer, fill your glass with cubed ice – this should be done at your bar station just before you start to make your cocktail. When your cocktail is complete and ready to be poured into the glass, discard the ice and any water in a sink, then follow the recipe's straining instructions to pour your cocktail into the chilled glass.

DILUTION

The addition of water in a cocktail. Spirits and other cocktail ingredients can be quite concentrated and complex in flavour, so the addition of water opens up the flavour profiles and helps to integrate all the

TECHNIQUES

The words and phrases below refer to specific cocktail-making techniques. If required, refer back to this list when it comes to making the cocktail recipes later in this book.

BUILD

A method of making a cocktail. 'Build in a glass' means that you make the cocktail directly in the glass it will be served in.

DASH

A dash is a small measure of liquid, normally used to measure bitters. It refers to one 'drop' of liquid that is shaken directly from the bitters bottle (or a dash bottle) into the cocktail. All recipes in this book refer to a dash directly from the original bitters bottle. Special dash bottles release less liquid, so increase the number of dashes by 25 per cent if using one.

DOUBLE STRAIN

An instruction to use a Hawthorne strainer and fine strainer together to strain the liquid from your tin or mixing glass into a serving glass. Double straining removes any fine shards of ice from the finished cocktail, avoiding any further dilution and ensuring your cocktail has a smooth texture. Note that cocktails containing egg white are not double strained, as this would break the foam that the egg white creates.

DRY SHAKE

The act of shaking a cocktail without ice in the shaker. This method is normally required when a cocktail uses egg white, as shaking without ice aids the formation of the foamy texture and head created by the egg white. See 'Shake' on page 34 for instructions.

GARNISH

The final touch and decoration of the cocktail. Garnishes are traditionally fruit or herbs but can be anything that is edible. A garnish normally adds aroma to a cocktail, giving it a second and important purpose.

HARD SHAKE

A hard shake is a style of shaking that requires power over a short space of time. The idea is to make the drink as cold and well mixed as possible without adding too much dilution. See 'Shake' on page 34 for instructions.

MUDDLE

In the case of herbs or fruit, muddling is the act of bruising an ingredient to extract its aroma, flavour and juice. Use the flat end of a cocktail spoon for muddling, or a special muddling tool that looks like a pestle but is made out of wood or plastic. Muddling can also be used to break down sugar cubes in a glass.

PRE-BATCH

The act of combining cocktail ingredients in advance of them being used. In essence, you are making parts of or whole cocktails in advance of them being served. The purpose is to simplify and speed up the cocktail-making process so that if you are serving a number of guests you can get a cocktail into a guest's hand in a shorter space of time. Depending on the recipe requirements, you may dilute your pre-batched cocktail before serving. This means that, when it comes to serving, particular attention needs to be paid to the temperature of the pre-batched cocktail, as you won't be stirring it over ice to chill the liquid down. Closely follow recipe instructions to ensure a perfect serve.

RINSE

A method of coating the inside of a glass, normally with a liqueur or strongly flavoured spirit, so that the flavour of the liquid but not its volume is added to the final cocktail. The benefit is the addition of flavour without changing the overall taste balance of the cocktail.

SERVE

The act of giving your guest a completed cocktail. When serving a drink, always hold the glass at the base and avoid touching the top half – your guest owns that part, as it is where they will drink from. Hygiene is the main consideration here, along with avoiding heat transfer from your hand to the liquid.

STIR

A method of combining, diluting and chilling ingredients in order to make a cocktail. Stirring is a very accurate way of diluting a cocktail, as you can easily monitor the level of dilution with a quick taste and continue to stir if more dilution is required. Stirring also produces a clear liquid. As the goal is to serve cold

and appropriately diluted drinks, when stirring, always hold the cocktail tin or mixing glass at the base, as this minimizes heat transfer from your hand.

You will notice that all stirred cocktail recipes in this book list the approximate number of stirs you will need. It's important to remember this is an approximation only – your ice, tools and room temperature will affect these requirements.

Follow the steps below.

1   Fill your cocktail tin or mixing glass with cubed ice.

2   Add the cocktail ingredients to the tin or glass, following your cocktail recipe.

3   Place a bar spoon, bowl end down, into the tin or mixing glass, ensuring the back of the spoon is flat against the inside wall of the vessel.

4   The goal is, as smoothly as possible, to rotate the ice

around the liquid; no ice cubes should be jumping around individually. The motion, in a sense, is a push and pull of the spoon around the circumference of the mixing vessel, while keeping the back of the spoon against the inside wall. To do this, hold the shaft of the spoon between your thumb and index finger; your middle finger is placed just under your index finger and your ring finger is placed on the same side as your thumb. Holding the spoon like this gives you enough resistance and control to use your fingers to rotate the spoon around the mixing vessel, keeping a push-and-pull motion in mind.

5   Stir the cocktail until mixed and diluted correctly. Your cocktail recipe will provide details of how many stirs you need, but do always take note of any environmental factors that may impact how many stirs are required, such as hot weather or lower-quality ice, which will dilute the drink more quickly. Taste the cocktail to check the dilution before serving.

SHAKE

Shaking is a cocktail-making method that is performed in a sealed cocktail shaker. It combines the ingredients, dilutes the liquid, chills and adds texture to a cocktail. A shaken cocktail will be cloudy when served.

There are various styles of cocktail shaking and some exist purely to add an element of showmanship to cocktail making. To make a shaken cocktail well, all you need to think about is moving the ice from one end of the tin to the other; this simple yet powerful movement mixes and dilutes consistently. Follow these steps below.

1   Place the larger tin from your cocktail shaker on a work surface and fill with cubed ice.

2   Add your cocktail ingredients to the smaller half of your cocktail shaker, then pour this mixture into the tin that is filled with ice.

3   Securely fit the smaller half of your tin into the larger half containing the liquid and ice. The two sides should fit snuggly together, creating a seal.

4   Pick the shaker up with one hand on top and the other hand underneath.

5   Shake the shaker in an up-and-down motion, paying attention to the feeling of the movement of the ice. It should feel like the cubes are moving from the top to the bottom of the shaker and back. Follow the instructions in the recipe to tell you how long to shake. With time and practice, you will start to notice a change in the sound the ice makes when the cocktail is ready.

To dry shake, follow the previous instructions from Step 2; essentially, it's the same process but with no ice. You will notice that the movement of the liquid will change when it is ready – it will feel like it has expanded and be softer as it moves. When you can feel the change, stop shaking. Ensuring the liquid is in the larger bottom half, carefully open the shaker and fill with ice. Then follow the previous instructions again from the beginning.

To hard shake, follow the previous instructions, but when it comes to the actual shaking of the sealed tin, do it with more power and over a shorter space of time – about half the time of a regular shake.

SINGLE STRAIN

An instruction to use just a Hawthorne strainer in the cocktail tin or mixing glass when straining your cocktail into the serving glass. Sour cocktails with egg white are commonly single strained, as this preserves the foam and texture within the liquid.

TASTE

In order to check that your cocktail is well made, you will need to taste it. This normally happens while the cocktail is still in the tin or glass so that if your drink requires more dilution you can continue to stir or shake it. The most professional and hygienic way is to use a disposable paper straw. For this method, place the straw in the liquid, holding it with your thumb and middle finger. Quickly tap your index finger over the top end of the straw; this pulls the liquid up the straw. Hold your index finger over the end of the straw and take the straw out of the drink. You will have drawn up and be holding a small amount of liquid in the straw. Place the wet end into your mouth and release your index finger to allow the liquid to flow out of the straw. Throw the straw away after use.

TOP UP

Normally, a cocktail is topped up with a fizzy mixer such as soda water or Champagne directly in the drinking glass, as we want to preserve the bubbles of these liquids. Essentially, you are pouring the fizzy liquid on top of the other cocktail ingredients until you reach the desired wash-line. This is done by eye and not necessarily measured with a jigger; attention must be paid to wash-lines otherwise cocktails can become over- or under-diluted (see the section about highball glasses on page 28 for more details). Topped-up drinks normally require a very gentle stir in the drinking glass to combine the fizzy liquid with the other ingredients, while maintaining the integrity of the bubbles and the fizz.

WASH-LINE

This is the level the liquid in a cocktail reaches in a drinking glass. The wash-line is normally somewhere between the rim of the glass and the width of one or two index fingers below the rim. The recipes in this book, where appropriate, will provide details on where the wash-line should be.

ORANGE SLICE

MINT SPRIG

**ORANGE PEEL
TWIST**

**LEMON PEEL
DISC**

OLIVES

**LEMON PEEL
TWIST**

**DISCARDED
ORANGE PEEL**

LIME WEDGE

TYPES OF GARNISH

DISC OF FRUIT PEEL

A small disc of citrus peel used to garnish a cocktail. To cut a fruit disc, follow the steps below.

1 Place your fruit on a chopping board, holding the fruit firmly in one hand.
2 Using your bar knife positioned at a 45-degree angle to the surface of the fruit, slice off a disc of fruit peel.

You will have some pith on the back of the peel. This is fine as it gives structure to the disc.

DISCARDED FRUIT PEEL

An instruction to garnish with a discarded fruit peel disc, usually citrus, requires you to cut a small disc of peel and express the oils from the peel over the surface of your cocktail. The disc is then thrown away and your drink is left with a fresh citrus scent.

To express the oils from a fruit peel, follow these steps.

1 Cut a disc of fruit peel (see left).
2 With the pith facing towards you, hold the disc between your thumb and index finger.
3 With your hand about 5cm (2in) above the surface of the cocktail and the skin side facing the liquid, gently squeeze the disc to express the citrus oils over the surface of your drink. Throw the disc away once the oils have been expressed.

LONG CITRUS PEEL

A 'long lemon', for example, refers to a long slice of lemon peel that is used to garnish a cocktail. Normally the peel measures 5–6cm (2–2½in), depending on the size of your glass, as the length should suit the glass. To cut a long lemon peel, follow the steps below.

1 Place your fruit on a chopping board, holding the fruit firmly in one hand.
2 Using your bar knife positioned at a 45-degree angle to the skin, slice a long strip of peel from the fruit. Depending on the length of garnish you need, this can be done from the top to the bottom of the fruit, or around the circumference of the fruit.
3 You will have some pith on the back of the peel – if excessive, cut some of this away by placing the peel flat on your chopping board with the pith side up. Holding your knife parallel to the board, carefully slice some of the pith away.
4 If desired, neaten up your long citrus peel by cutting it into the shape of a long parallelogram.

SLICE

This normally refers to a precise slice of citrus fruit with an even thickness. A slice is normally semicircular in shape, but if the fruit is small, it can be a whole slice, also known as a 'wheel'. If your drinking glass is too small, you may wish to cut the semicircle in half again to create a quadrant wedge. This is also useful if using larger fruits such as oranges or grapefruits. To cut a fruit slice, follow these steps.

1   Place your fruit on its side on a chopping board, holding the fruit firmly in one hand.
2   Using your bar knife at an angle of 90 degrees to your fruit, slice the fruit into 5mm (¼in) slices.
3   Remove any pips from the slices and cut each slice in half or quarters if you require a smaller slice for your cocktail glass.

TWIST OF CITRUS PEEL

A long, thin piece of citrus peel, usually 6cm (2½in) by 1cm (½in), twisted to create a coil shape. The twist is then balanced on the edge of the drinking glass or across the ice inside the glass. To cut a twist, follow the steps below.

1   Follow the steps on page 37 to cut a long citrus peel.
2   Hold one end of the long citrus peel in each of your hands.
3   Twist your hands in opposite directions. The long citrus peel should coil up like a spring. When you release your hands, the peel should relax a little but stay in a coiled shape.
4   Balance your citrus twist on the edge of your cocktail glass or on top of the ice on the surface of your cocktail.

WEDGE

A segment of citrus fruit that has been cut into a wedge shape. A wedge includes the peel and flesh of the fruit. To cut a wedge, follow these steps.

1   Place your fruit on a chopping board and use a bar knife to cut the fruit in half lengthways.
2   Take one half and place on the chopping board cut side down.
3   Working from one side of the fruit to the other, cut the fruit into even wedges, angling the cuts to the centre of the cut side.
4   Remove any pips from the fruit and any pith that may be running down the edge of the flesh.

HERB SPRIG

A single branch of a herb, including the leaves, usually around 10–12cm (4–4½in) in length.

SALT RIM

Covering the rim of a glass with sea salt flakes – Maldon salt is ideal. You can prepare salt-rimmed glasses in advance, saving on time when making your cocktails. To make a salt rim, follow the steps below.

1   First cut a fresh wedge of citrus, matching the wedge to the citrus you will use in the cocktail.

2   Run the flesh of the citrus fruit around the outside rim of the glass, aiming for an even and straight layer of juice up to 5mm (¼in) below the rim of the glass.

3   Spread out a handful of sea salt flakes on a small plate. Roll the moist rim of the glass in the salt, which should stick to the glass and create a neat and dense salt rim.

SUGAR RIM

Covering the rim of a glass with sugar – caster sugar is ideal. You can prepare sugar-rimmed glasses in advance, saving on time when making your cocktails. To make a sugar rim, follow the previous steps for a salt rim, swapping the salt for sugar.

CHAPTER 4:
BASIC INGREDIENTS

Exploring the breadth and quality of cocktail ingredients available to us can be exciting – there are so many quality products we can choose to use in our cocktails to ensure they suit our tastes and needs. However, it can also be quite daunting figuring out which products are worth investing in, especially if you're on a budget.

Versatility is a key consideration. A versatile product will be balanced in flavour, meeting your requirements in a functional way. As balanced products have the potential to work in a selection of cocktails in a range of different categories, they will become the backbone of your spirit collection; all other products pivot around them, depending on your flavour moods and desires. These products also work as springboards for trying different cocktail recipes with the ingredients you have to hand.

The following list of ingredients is just a starting point. I've highlighted what I feel to be the most versatile products, suitable for use across many different cocktail categories, so that you can maximize these ingredients. First you need to pick your starting point – refer back to Chapter 1 on how to approach cocktail making and the key foundations we set. You may wish to start by exploring a favourite spirit or style of cocktail and refer to what is required from there on, looking at your most versatile options so you can branch out into different cocktail categories when you're ready.

Some of the ingredients in this chapter can easily be made at home. I've noted where this is possible, but if you have a commercial product you'd like to use instead, then please do use it.

VODKA

A well-made vodka should be smooth with no excessive alcohol burn, chemical taste or aroma. Vodkas made from wheat, rye, potato and, in some cases, rice are readily available, with wheat and rye producing the most versatile products. Personally, I like rye vodka, as it provides a warm, creamy flavour that produces clean and smooth cocktails. Potato-based vodkas may have a more distinct flavour profile, so do take that into account if you're looking to explore this style of vodka. Rice-based vodka is less common, but the Japanese vodka listed below is a good example and offers a smooth and delicate experience.

KEY CHARACTERISTICS OF A VERSATILE VODKA:
Smooth and clean flavour.

TYPICAL ABV: 40%

COCKTAIL CATEGORIES: Stirred, sour, long.

WYBOROWA ORIGINAL

40% ABV, Polish rye vodka.

NOSE: Creamy, slightly nutty, toasted rye.

PALATE: Rye leads with an almost wholemeal bread-like quality, and evolves into a slightly sweet taste with a hint of mineral.

TEXTURE: Smooth, warm and creamy.

STYLE: Classic and creamy.

ABSOLUT ELYX

....

42.3% ABV, Swedish luxury
single-estate vodka.

NOSE: A warm and clean scent
with a touch of cereal.

PALATE: Clean and light
mineral taste.

TEXTURE: Very smooth
and clean.

STYLE: Luxury vodka that focuses
on the locality of its wheat and
copper distillation techniques.

BELVEDERE

....

40% ABV, Polish luxury
rye vodka.

NOSE: Creamy, soft rye notes.

PALATE: Sweet and mineral,
almost savoury.

TEXTURE: Creamy yet clean,
smooth texture.

STYLE: Luxury vodka that focuses
on the terroir of its ingredients
and the heritage of Polish vodka.

HAKU

....

40% ABV, Japanese rice-
based vodka.

NOSE: Subtle milky notes.

PALATE: Sweet, creamy, almost
rice pudding-like with a refined
mineral finish.

TEXTURE: Light, soft
and rounded.

STYLE: Contemporary, focusing
on the qualities of its ingredients
and filtration.

GIN

If you are only able to buy one gin, a classic London dry gin is a great place to start. I find Beefeater to be one of the most balanced and versatile on the market; it produces great results in all gin cocktails. The world of gin is huge: if you can, do try others to build your palate's knowledge and find your personal preference.

KEY CHARACTERISTICS OF A VERSATILE GIN: Balanced juniper, citrus and woody notes.

TYPICAL ABV: 40%

COCKTAIL CATEGORIES: Champagne, stirred, bitter, sour, long.

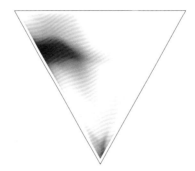

BEEFEATER LONDON DRY GIN
....

40% ABV, nine botanicals (juniper, lemon peel, Seville orange peel, almond, angelica root, coriander seed, angelica seed, orris root, liquorice root).

NOSE: Citrus and coriander seed, with a note of juniper tying it all together.

PALATE: Upfront citrus with a juniper backbone that as a whole mellows out to a subtle almond and woody finish.

TEXTURE: Rich and smooth.

STYLE: Classic but equally complex. Great overall balance between the citrus, juniper and wood in this gin.

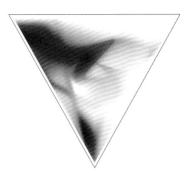

TANQUERAY LONDON DRY GIN
....

43.1% ABV, four botanicals (juniper, angelica root, coriander seed, liquorice root).

NOSE: Juniper, backed up by coriander.

PALATE: Juniper and coriander seed lead, evolving into an overall effect of fresh pine.

TEXTURE: Clean, precise, slightly spicy.

STYLE: Classic, clean and dry juniper-led gin.

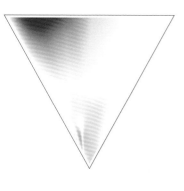

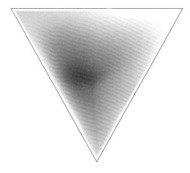

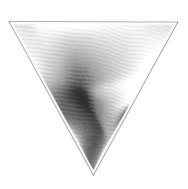

SIPSMITH LONDON DRY GIN

41.6% ABV, ten botanicals (juniper, coriander seed, angelica root, liquorice root, orris root, almond, cassia bark, cinnamon, Seville orange peel, lemon peel).

NOSE: Juniper, citrus, green wood.

PALATE: Woody juniper with bright citrus that evolves into an aromatic green finish.

TEXTURE: A well-integrated gin that is smooth and in a sense gentle in its presentation of flavour.

STYLE: Traditional yet forward thinking with its balance of zesty bright notes that evolve into a more mellow resinous flavour.

PLYMOUTH LONDON DRY GIN

41.2% ABV, seven botanicals (juniper, coriander seed, orange peel, lemon peel, angelica root, green cardamom, orris root).

NOSE: Juniper, citrus and coriander seed.

PALATE: Green notes followed by juniper and citrus, evolving into warm gentle wood.

TEXTURE: Smooth, almost soft in its texture.

STYLE: Classic, balanced and gentle.

ROKU GIN

43% ABV, six contemporary botanicals that build upon the classic juniper structure of gin (sakura flower, sakura leaf, yuzu peel, sencha tea, gyokuro tea, sansho pepper).

NOSE: Floral, herbal, pepper.

PALATE: Floral and bright, slipping into herbaceous pepper and juniper notes with a woody and citrus finish.

TEXTURE: Bold yet delicate, smooth and clean.

STYLE: Contemporary, delicate and aromatic.

WHISKY

There are many different styles and types of whisky available for us to explore, each with its own technicalities in production and ultimately unique flavour profile. To keep this section of our ingredients list focused and practical, I have selected products that I feel offer a balanced and versatile approach suited to cocktail making.

KEY CHARACTERISTICS OF A VERSATILE WHISKY: A light Scotch and a sweet Bourbon will prove most useful across the cocktail categories.

TYPICAL ABV: 40–45%

COCKTAIL CATEGORIES: Stirred, bitter, sour, long.

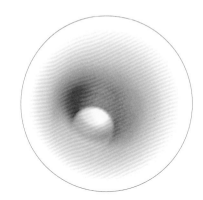

JOHNNIE WALKER BLACK LABEL
....

40% ABV, a 12-year-old blended Scotch whisky.

NOSE: Caramel, vanilla, slightly smoky toasted grain nose.

PALATE: Clean, creamy and slightly sweet toasted grain flavour that evolves into a slightly dry, smoky finish.

TEXTURE: Smooth and silky, evolving into a subtle peppery heat.

STYLE: A balanced sweet and smoke flavour make this a versatile Scotch whisky.

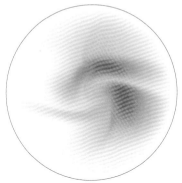

SUNTORY WHISKY TOKI
....

43% ABV, a blended Japanese whisky.

NOSE: Light, green, clean, slightly creamy grain nose.

PALATE: Peppery heat that evolves into a honeyed melon sweetness.

TEXTURE: Delicate yet precise.

STYLE: Light and subtle, making this product perfect for light whisky cocktails such as a Whisky Highball (see page 203).

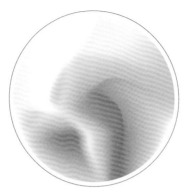

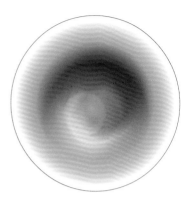

BUFFALO TRACE KENTUCKY STRAIGHT BOURBON

40% ABV, made from a mixture of corn, rye and barley malt. Aged in new oak barrels.

NOSE: Spiced orange, vanilla and oak on the nose.

PALATE: Vanilla-soaked oranges, combined with a rounded toasted grain note that evolves into a sweet toffee finish.

TEXTURE: Rich with a touch of dryness that cuts through on the palate.

STYLE: Classic and balanced, an incredibly versatile Bourbon.

MAKER'S MARK KENTUCKY STRAIGHT BOURBON

45% ABV, made using soft red winter wheat, corn and malted barley. No rye is used in Maker's Mark. Aged in seasoned and charred American white oak barrels.

NOSE: Citrus and spice with a gentle butterscotch nose.

PALATE: Subtle orange with a touch of lemon that combines with soft and sweet caramel.

TEXTURE: Smooth and silky first impression that evolves into a peppery dry finish.

STYLE: Despite its higher ABV, this is a lighter style of Bourbon that opens up well in cocktails.

RITTENHOUSE STRAIGHT RYE WHISKY

50% ABV, made using predominantly rye, corn and malted barley. Aged for four years.

NOSE: Toasted rye, spice and oak on the nose.

PALATE: Deep and rich rye bread notes with a spiced oak finish.

TEXTURE: Rich and thick on the palate with a gentle heat.

STYLE: Classic rye-focused whisky with great body and length.

RUM

A lightly aged white rum, known as a light rum, will prove most useful in cocktails. If you are looking to explore rum cocktails in more detail, look at your recipe requirements and invest in a golden and dark rum if needed. The example rums here are Cuban, as they are most appropriate to the recipes in this book.

KEY CHARACTERISTICS OF A VERSATILE LIGHT OR DARK RUM: While both warm and gentle in flavour, a light rum should have complexity with a bright fruity note. A dark rum will be deeper and richer in flavour with a stronger molasses taste. A more premium golden rum is in the middle of these two products, and can prove useful for certain classic cocktails.

TYPICAL ABV: 40%

COCKTAIL CATEGORIES: Champagne, stirred, sour, long.

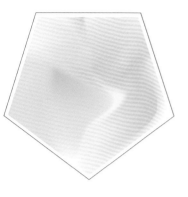
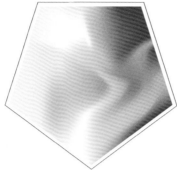
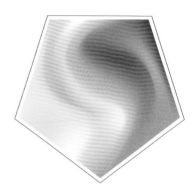

HAVANA CLUB 3 AÑOS

40% ABV, Cuban white rum made from sugar-cane molasses and aged for three years.

NOSE: Juicy, green, pineapple and fresh banana notes.

PALATE: Green sugar cane that evolves into tropical fruits and banana.

TEXTURE: Bright, fresh and juicy on the palate.

STYLE: Classic Cuban rum that is ideal for cocktails.

HAVANA CLUB 7 AÑOS

40% ABV, matured in old Bourbon barrels for seven years.

NOSE: Rich molasses and dried fruits with a touch of oak.

PALATE: Molasses and tobacco, softened by sweet dried tropical fruits.

TEXTURE: Rich and smooth.

STYLE: Classic dark Cuban rum that works well on its own over ice or in cocktails.

HAVANA CLUB SELECCIÓN DE MAESTROS

45% ABV, showcases the finest of Havana's rums. Casks are hand selected, then bottled at a higher ABV for a more intense and flavoursome rum experience.

NOSE: Toasted pecan, caramel, candied fruits.

PALATE: Caramelized pineapple and citrus that evolve into a warm cocoa and gentle spiced oak finish.

TEXTURE: Rich and smooth, slightly spicy dry feel.

STYLE: A premium aged golden Cuban rum that works well in classic stirred cocktails that need a rum with a little more depth of structure.

AGAVE SPIRITS

There are three key products in this group that offer a good place for us to start. The first is blanco or silver tequila made with blue agave, which should be familiar to you, as it is commonly used in Margaritas and proves most useful across the cocktail categories. This tequila is usually unaged or aged for less than two months, meaning its flavour stays bright and bold. The second product is an aged reposado tequila, which is well worth exploring, especially if you are looking to make a more spirit-focused tequila cocktail. Here, the tequila has been rested in oak for at least two months and up to one year. This ageing process gives us a woody and soft vanilla flavour that provides us with a little more structure to work with, as well as making a tequila that is more suitable for sipping.

Finally, I have listed a mezcal for you to explore. Mezcal, just like tequila, is an agave-based spirit, but it can be made from many different types of agave, with the choice of plant and how it is processed giving us a variety of flavour profiles. Because of the way the agave is cooked, mezcal tends to have a more smoky flavour profile than tequila. But by no means should you think that mezcal is just a smoky tequila – this product really showcases the qualities of different agave plants, the terroir of the land and the producer's style. Mezcal made from espadin has a slightly sweet, mild and modest flavour. I find the smoky notes of this liquid gentle and approachable, offering a balanced introduction and starting point to this style of spirit. Mezcal can be fun to explore if agave's flavours and traditions excite you.

KEY CHARACTERISTICS OF A VERSATILE AGAVE SPIRIT: Clean and precise with no chemical notes. Look for 100% pure agave for the best-quality products.

TYPICAL ABV: 38–45%

COCKTAIL CATEGORIES: Champagne, stirred, bitter, sour, long.

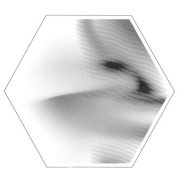
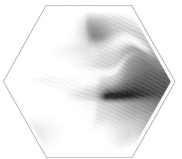
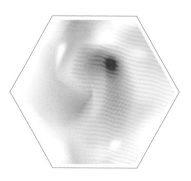

OCHO BLANCO TEQUILA

40% ABV, single-estate silver tequila, made from 100% pure agave.

NOSE: A green, almost savoury nose that gives an impression of juiciness.

PALATE: Complex agave which evolves into a drier wood note.

TEXTURE: Almost oily mouthfeel, rich with a smooth heat.

STYLE: Smooth and balanced.

TAPATIO TEQUILA REPOSADO

38% ABV, made with 100% agave. Aged in old Bourbon casks for four months.

NOSE: Almost lactic, with a green apple note to give a savoury impression on the nose.

PALATE: Resinous agave with a slight peppery note that softens into oak.

TEXTURE: Silky and smooth with a rounded creamy mouthfeel, balanced by a touch of dryness.

STYLE: Restrained and smooth, yet complex.

MEZCAL AMORES ESPADIN

41% ABV, artisanal mezcal made from 100% espadin agave.

NOSE: Resinous smoke that is almost floral and sweet on the nose.

PALATE: Bright, clean and alive with heat. Once the first impression of the alcohol passes, notes of green herb and clean citrus remain.

TEXTURE: Spicy, clean and resinous.

STYLE: Mild and modest, yet impactful.

COGNAC

Cognac is not used as extensively as other dark spirits in this book. However, it has its place in some of the most classic of cocktails. Though totally unique in its flavour profile, I feel the structure of this liquid sits somewhere between that of Bourbon and golden aged rums.

KEY CHARACTERISTICS OF A VERSATILE COGNAC:
Smooth with a gentle and warm fruit flavour.

TYPICAL ABV: 40%

COCKTAIL CATEGORIES: Champagne, stirred, sour, long.

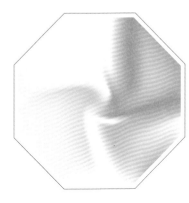

MERLET BROTHERS BLEND VSOP

40% ABV, made using a blend of Fins Bois and Grande Champagne *crus* eaux-de-vie that are aged for a minimum of four years in a barrel.

NOSE: Sweet orange and dried apricots with a delicate smooth wood nose.

PALATE: Aromatic dried fruits that evolve into a honeyed sweetness with a touch of spice.

TEXTURE: Silky, smooth and subtle.

STYLE: A modern yet balanced Cognac, making this a versatile option for classic cocktails.

ABSINTHE

Often mistaken as a liqueur, absinthe is actually a highly aromatized and distinctive spirit. It is not a spirit that will suit everyone's taste, but if you are inclined to the strong herbal, aniseed flavour of this spirit, you may like to explore its use in cocktails.

KEY CHARACTERISTICS OF A VERSATILE ABSINTHE:
Clean and green herbal flavour profile that produces precise and bright results.

TYPICAL ABV: 65–70%

COCKTAIL CATEGORIES: Champagne, stirred.

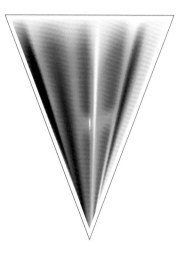

PERNOD ABSINTHE

68% ABV, a historical absinthe made to a traditional recipe.

NOSE: Green aniseed and liquorice with an almost candied citrus note.

PALATE: Powerful aniseed, green herbs and liquorice sweetness.

TEXTURE: Oily mouthfeel with a cooling start and warming finish on the palate.

STYLE: A classic absinthe with a balanced flavour profile.

COCKTAIL BITTERS

The 'seasoning' in a cocktail, cocktail bitters are available in a range of flavours from supermarkets and specialist cocktail suppliers. I have included the most universally used bitters here. These products have a long shelf life, so it's useful to keep a small selection to hand.

KEY CHARACTERISTICS: Though all cocktail bitters taste bitter and are aromatic, their flavour profiles can vary from the deep and woody to the light and fruity. Refer to your cocktail recipe and select the required bitters.

TYPICAL ABV: 28–45%

COCKTAIL CATEGORIES: Champagne, stirred, sour, long.

ANGOSTURA BITTERS

The most iconic and classic cocktail bitters that prove useful in a wide range of cocktails. No matter where you start on your cocktail journey, always have a bottle of Angostura bitters to hand.

NOSE: Clove, nutmeg and cinnamon notes create an overall warm spice nose.

PALATE: Clove evolves into a warming spice, dry wood and gentian note with a bitter-tasting finish.

TEXTURE: Palate-stimulating through its bitter taste.

STYLE: Classic, with a balanced bitter flavour profile.

PEYCHAUD'S BITTERS

These bright pink-red bitters prove useful in the more lightly aromatic classic cocktails.

NOSE: A medicinal nose with notes of aniseed and candied citrus.

PALATE: A brighter-pitched bitterness that is herbal and almost floral in flavour.

TEXTURE: Clean and light with a gentle bitterness on the palate.

STYLE: Highly aromatic, more than just a bitter taste.

ORANGE BITTERS

There are various orange bitters on the market. The most important quality to look for is a clean and refined citrus note with a bitter finish. I find Angostura Orange to have a bright and strong orange note. Other widely available brands will provide more spice, if that is something you prefer.

NOSE: Fresh orange peel nose.

PALATE: Bright, juicy orange peel that slips into a more spiced orange finish.

TEXTURE: Juicy and lightly bitter on the palate.

STYLE: Juicy citrus-led bitters.

GRAPEFRUIT BITTERS

As with orange bitters, grapefruit bitters should be dry and bright with a lighter citrus and slightly woody aroma that is often found in grapefruit. I find Bittermens Hopped Grapefruit Bitters a good example.

NOSE: Fresh grapefruit peel with an almost perfumed note.

PALATE: Bright, dry grapefruit peel, moving into a dry and precise bitter taste.

TEXTURE: Sharp and precise on the palate.

STYLE: Dry citrus bitters.

BOKER'S BITTERS

A unique and more specialist type of cocktail bitters, Boker's bitters are based on historical recipes and used in some classic cocktails, specifically the Martinez (see page 115).

NOSE: Bright with notes of dry citrus and green cardamom that give a fresh impression.

PALATE: The freshness of green cardamon evolves into a dry bitterness that lingers. Warm, subtle spice gives a little body to the overall taste.

TEXTURE: Dry and precise on the palate.

STYLE: A clean and focused style of bitters.

LIQUEURS

Generally speaking, a liqueur is a spirit that has a fruity or herbal flavour and has also had sugar added to it, meaning there is a perceivable sweetness to this liquid. A crème liqueur will contain more sugar than a standard liqueur. I have listed a selection of products here that may prove useful to you.

CAMPARI

A bitter-sweet Italian liqueur that forms the cornerstone of Italian bitter cocktails. Campari's recipe is a secret, though we do know it contains a wide range of herbs, flowers, bitter woods and citrus peels.

TYPICAL ABV: 25%

COCKTAIL CATEGORIES: Bitter.

APEROL

Another bitter-sweet Italian liqueur that forms the basis for the popular Aperol Spritz (see page 149). Though still bitter, it is a little sweeter than Campari and has a fruitier rhubarb note in its flavour profile.

TYPICAL ABV: 11%

COCKTAIL CATEGORIES: Bitter.

TRIPLE SEC

My preferred brand of this orange-flavoured liqueur is Merlet Trois Citrus. It utilizes three types of citrus – bitter orange, blood orange and lemon – to create a complex and bright triple sec liqueur.

TYPICAL ABV: 40%

COCKTAIL CATEGORIES: Stirred, sour, long.

MARASCHINO LIQUEUR

Luxardo Maraschino Liqueur is a quality product made from Marasca cherries. It's rich and fruity in flavour with hints of almond.

TYPICAL ABV: 32%

COCKTAIL CATEGORIES: Stirred, sour.

AMARETTO

This roasted and nutty almond-based liqueur has a distinctive flavour profile and forms the basis for one of the most iconic sour cocktails, the Amaretto Sour (see page 176). Some Amarettos are made using apricot and cherry stones, as well as almonds. Try to find a less sweet Amaretto with a clear roasted-almond flavour. Bepi Tosolini Saliza Amaretto is a good option.

TYPICAL ABV: 25–30%

COCKTAIL CATEGORIES: Sour.

CREME DE CASSIS

Merlet produce a high-quality, traditional crème de cassis; it's rich in blackcurrant flavour, yet manages to be clean and precise. A perfect option for cocktails.

TYPICAL ABV: 20%

COCKTAIL CATEGORIES: Champagne, long.

FRUIT LIQUEURS

In general, fruit liqueurs are useful products to have to hand and can be used to explore personal flavour preferences. I find that Merlet produces one of the strongest and most consistent of ranges. Their heritage of fruit growing and Cognac and liqueur production really shows in the quality of their products.

TYPICAL ABV: 18–20%

COCKTAIL CATEGORIES: Champagne, sour, long.

WINES

Wine is a world in its own right and something that is not within the scope of this book. But I do want to touch on a few key considerations when using wines in cocktails.

CHAMPAGNE

The slightly drier profile of brut Champagne creates the most balanced, sweet-to-acid taste profile in a cocktail. As for aromatic profile, this is down to personal preference. Lighter and fresher Champagnes with notes of green and summer stone fruits will work well across a range of cocktails. Warmer Champagnes with biscuit notes equally have a place and will produce great results too. Don't feel you need to spend a fortune buying Champagne. While the larger houses produce liquid of amazing quality and consistency, smaller producers also have skill and can produce a quality product. I purchased a budget bottle of Champagne from a supermarket and it worked incredibly well in cocktails.

TYPICAL ABV: 12%

COCKTAIL CATEGORIES: Champagne.

PROSECCO

This Italian sparkling wine proves useful in aperitivo bitter cocktails. Look for a Prosecco with a bright green aroma and clean finish. A Prosecco that is more acidic than sweet will balance better against bitter-sweet Italian liqueurs.

TYPICAL ABV: 12%

COCKTAIL CATEGORIES: Bitter.

RED WINE

A juicy red wine with a gentle tannic structure will prove most useful when working with cocktails. Anything that is too distinctive will risk throwing off the balance of the cocktail.

TYPICAL ABV: 11–14%

COCKTAIL CATEGORIES: Sour.

VERMOUTH

Vermouth is a fortified wine that has been aromatized with a selection of botanicals. The result is a liquid with a complex flavour profile; herbal, citrus and floral notes all play a part here, along with bitter woods and spices.

Vermouth is a key ingredient in classic cocktails. At some point in your cocktail journey, it is worth exploring a few different options to find your favourite.

DRY VERMOUTH

Made from a white wine base, this style of vermouth is clean, bright and dry. It's most commonly used in Martinis. I find Dolin Dry Vermouth de Chambéry to be a balanced option and a good place to start.

TYPICAL ABV: 15–18%

COCKTAIL CATEGORIES:
Stirred, sour.

SWEET VERMOUTH

Traditionally made from a red wine base, sweet vermouth is warm, rich and fruity with an approachable bitter taste. This complex vermouth is diverse and will work with a wide range of spirits in cocktails. Carpano produces a range of sweet vermouths that balance well in cocktails.

TYPICAL ABV: 16%

COCKTAIL CATEGORIES:
Stirred, bitter.

SYRUPS

Syrups play a key part in cocktails – they offer a way for us to add sweetness in a very controlled manner. In some cases, a syrup will also bring additional flavour to a cocktail. While you can buy most syrups, they are also easy to make at home – I've included some recipes here. If you do buy syrups, look for the best quality you can and avoid products with unnecessary ingredients such as thickeners.

SUGAR SYRUP

This is a must for cocktail making, the basic syrup we will use in our cocktails. If buying sugar syrup, look for a pure sugar-cane syrup. If you'd like to make it at home, follow the steps below.

1   To make 500ml (17oz) of syrup, place 400g (14oz) of white caster sugar in a heatproof bowl.

2   Add 200ml (6⅔oz) of hot water to the bowl – this can be water heated in a kettle.

3   Stir to fully dissolve the sugar into the water.

4   Store your syrup in a sealed bottle in the fridge – it should be stable for a week.

AGAVE SYRUP

Agave syrup is made from the juice of agave plants and, due to its shared flavour profile, is mainly used in tequila- and mezcal-based cocktails. You can buy agave syrup from most health food shops; you will then need to prepare the syrup for use in cocktails. Diluting your purchased agave syrup makes it easier to work with and produces a sweetness level that is more balanced for use in the cocktails in this book.

1   To make 300ml (10oz) of prepared syrup, measure out 200ml (6⅔oz) of bought agave syrup in a heatproof jug.

2   Add 100ml (3⅓oz) of hot water to the jug – this can be water heated in a kettle.

3   Stir to fully dissolve the agave syrup into the water.

4   Store your syrup in a sealed bottle in the fridge and use the same day.

GRENADINE

Grenadine is a syrup made with pomegranate juice. Although you can purchase this syrup, I like to make it from juice and sugar, as I feel the result is much cleaner in flavour. Look in your local health food shop for good-quality pomegranate juice.

1   To make 300ml (10oz) of syrup, place 200g (7oz) of white caster sugar in a mixing bowl.

2   Add 200ml (6⅔oz) of pomegranate juice to the bowl.

3   Stir to fully dissolve the sugar into the pomegranate juice.

4   Store your syrup in a sealed bottle in the fridge – it should be stable for a week.

RASPBERRY SYRUP

I like to use pre-made raspberry syrup and this is mainly for consistency reasons. Fresh fruit is variable in flavour, which can be an issue for us if we are looking to serve consistent-tasting cocktails. When selecting a raspberry syrup, look for the best quality you can find. That said, if in the summer months you have excess raspberries to hand, look up a recipe for homemade raspberry syrup and enjoy a Clover Club (see page 181).

ORGEAT

Orgeat is an almond-based syrup. As there are so many high-quality nut milks now available to purchase, I suggest you make your own. Do look for an almond milk without thickeners, as this will change the texture of the syrup.

1   To make 475ml (16oz) of orgeat, place 350g (12⅓oz) of white caster sugar in a mixing bowl.

2   Add 250ml (8½oz) of almond milk to the bowl.

3   Stir to fully dissolve the sugar into the almond milk.

4   Add 2.5ml (½ tsp) of orange blossom water to the syrup and stir to combine.

5   Store your syrup in a sealed bottle in the fridge – it should be stable for a week.

HONEY SYRUP

Honey is used in a small selection of cocktails, such as the Airmail. As with agave syrup, honey should be diluted to make it more palatable and easier to work with. Refer to page 96 for the recipe.

CORDIALS

I define a cordial as a flavoured syrup that also contains acid. A cordial is normally concentrated and needs to be diluted before being consumed. Cordials are useful in cocktails, as they provide aroma along with sweetness and acid, creating a balanced overall flavour in cocktails such as the Gimlet (see page 109). Although we only use lime cordial in this book, you can explore all sorts of flavours through using cordials. It is now quite easy to find high-quality cordials in supermarkets as well as from more specialist food suppliers. You may also like to explore making your own.

FRUIT AND JUICES

In the world of cocktails, citrus is generally used in two ways: as a garnish where we need the peel from the fruit, and as an acidifier, which is when we need the juice. If you are buying fruit for its peel, make sure the fruit is unwaxed. When it comes to citrus juice, I recommend buying fresh fruit and juicing it; the results will taste brighter. Fresh juice will be at its best within 24 hours of being squeezed.

If you do purchase juices, try to find the best quality you can and test it in a cocktail before you serve it to a guest. Take note of the sweetness and sourness of the juice to ensure balance and follow any specific suggestions below. Finally, if you find a brand of juice that suits you, stick with it to help keep your cocktails consistent.

As with bought orange juice, if you decide to buy grapefruit juice, check the balance in your selected cocktail and add a little sugar if necessary.

CRANBERRY JUICE

I find the best cranberry juices are sold in health food shops. These juices tend to be stronger in overall cranberry flavour; to me, supermarket brands have a more generic 'red fruit' flavour. Cranberry juice is very variable across brands, so if you find a juice that suits you, stick with it.

TOMATO JUICE

This is the key ingredient in a Bloody Mary (see page 204). It's now possible to buy really high-quality tomato juices designed specifically for use in a Bloody Mary and the great news is these juices can normally be found in supermarkets. You will see that such juices tend to contain spices and seasoning already, which is convenient. If you are a Bloody Mary fan, look out for these products and try a selection to find your favourite.

LEMONS AND LIMES

Lemons and limes are used for their juice in cocktails; the fruit and peel are used as garnishes. One lemon will give you approximately 40ml (1⅓oz) of juice. One lime will give you approximately 30ml (1oz) of juice.

ORANGES

Oranges are used for their juice in cocktails; the fruit and peel are used as garnishes. One large orange will give you approximately 70ml (2⅓oz) of juice.

If purchasing orange juice, taste to check the sweetness and acid balance. I often find supermarket juices to be more acidic in taste, so you may wish to add a little sugar to them before using. Balance this to your preference.

PINK GRAPEFRUITS

Pink grapefruits are used for their juice in cocktails; the fruit and zest are used as garnishes. One grapefruit will give you approximately 200ml (6⅔oz) of juice.

OTHER INGREDIENTS

The following ingredients are used for specific purposes in certain cocktails. Some, such as eggs, may be an ingredient you always have to hand in your kitchen. Others, such as verjus, can be used as an alternative souring agent in a cocktail and have a long shelf life. I've included a few considerations when selecting and working with these ingredients.

EGG WHITES

Egg whites are mainly used in sour cocktails to create the foam some of these drinks require. If making one of these cocktails, ensure your egg whites are fresh and be aware of any dietary requirements of your guests – it may not be appropriate to use raw egg white for some. You can use pasteurized egg whites, which are purchased in a carton. The only difference is that there will be a little less foam and it will hold for a shorter space of time.

EGG-FREE FOAMING AGENTS

Available to purchase online, products like Ms. Better's Bitters Miraculous Foamer are worth having to hand as an egg white replacement in cocktails. A few drops are added to a cocktail, it is dry shaken, then shaken with ice, and will produce a quality foam. A little research may turn up other similar products.

VERJUS

A lightly acidic, slightly sweet vinegar that is made from the juice of pressed red or white grapes. Verjus is a useful product to have to hand if you need an acidifying agent to replace lemon or lime juice. Its gentle acid taste profile and slightly green fruity aromatic profile tend to balance well in cocktails. Verjus is traditionally used in food as a deglazing agent or in vinaigrettes and sauces, making it a useful product to have to hand.

OLIVES

Good-quality, unflavoured olives are essential if you are planning to serve Martinis. As to the type and style, a green olive is the classic option, but ultimately this choice is down to your preference. If stored in oil, give the olives a quick rinse before use or you will notice drops of oil floating on top of your drink. If making a Dirty Martini (see pages 107 and 113), you'll need to ensure that your olives come in brine, not oil.

SILVER SKIN PICKLED ONIONS

Silver skin pickled onions are a key ingredient in a Gibson (see page 108). For best results, find the smallest cocktail onions, as their size suits the drink. If these aren't available, go with the smallest silver skin pickled onions you can find, ensuring they are in a sour rather than sweet vinegar.

TEAS

When it comes to the later stages in this book and bespoke recipe development, having a selection of high-quality black and green loose-leaf teas will prove useful; the tannic structure of tea, along with its roasted and/or bright aromatic profile, works very well in cocktails. Teas have a long shelf life and will keep for use in cocktails, but if you don't get to that stage you can just brew them and enjoy them on their own. I've enjoyed discovering the world of Korean tea through a really unique supplier called Be-oom. If you are interested in tea or would like to explore its uses in cocktails, then I suggest investigating what is available to you from smaller as well as larger suppliers.

GROUND COFFEE

If you are partial to an Espresso Martini (see page 214), ensure you have quality ground coffee to hand. The market has recently boomed, with niche coffee roasters producing distinctive coffees that you can explore in a cocktail. For me, balance in flavour is key, and as someone who does not have specialist coffee-making equipment at home, I'm excited by a new group of producers who are bridging the gap between quality and convenience. Artisan Coffee Co are leading the way in that section of the coffee world and are worth exploring if, like mine, your coffee-making set-up is very simple. Look into your locally available options and adjust your coffee set-up – perhaps grinding beans at home might be something you'd like to explore.

MIXERS

A selection of mixers such as soda water, tonic water, ginger beer and ginger ale are useful to have stored away, ready for use. I like the fact that a lot of these products now come in small individual-serve cans. If I'm only making one or two drinks, I don't have to waste a large bottle of mixer.

Although we don't use tonic water in any recipes in this book, it's worth having a few cans or bottles stored away. If you are hosting and need to serve a quick drink while you are busy, a gin and tonic will always satisfy a guest and buy you time.

CHAPTER 5:
THE FIVE BASIC TASTES AND MORE

Sweet, sour, bitter, salt and umami are the basic tastes we are familiar with. We know that when combined correctly, these tastants – along with aroma – create delicious food. A food point of view provides us with a starting point for our approach to cocktail making – however, there is more to a glass of liquid than meets the eye. You might like to read this chapter with a drink to hand, whether it's a cocktail, a glass of wine or something non-alcoholic. Go grab yourself something to sip and consider while we discuss what a cocktail is and how it works.

Compared to a drink, a plate of food provides you with a lot of choice. You can choose which ingredient to eat first and which other ingredients to combine with it. At any point, you can decide to change the order and combination in which you eat the different elements. You can savour a particular component; who else keeps their Yorkshire puddings until last? All of this means that you can personalize and dramatically change your experience as you eat. A drink, in its most simple form, is a liquid contained in and enjoyed from a single glass. The flavours held within that glass are presented as a whole; you can't choose to change your experience halfway through or save a part of the drink until last (unless you like an olive in your Martini – we'll come back to that later). Apart from a slight temperature increase, or a little extra dilution if the drink is served over ice, the liquid's profile is ultimately the same from start to finish. Take note as you sip your drink while reading: how different is your first sip to your last?

When we make or consume a cocktail, we are providing or committing to a fixed experience, and this changes our relationship with a drink. Mood, preference, structure and mechanics need to be considered before a cocktail is made. This might sound complex, but ultimately you are taking the role of a host, curating an offering that is suited to you and your guests. You would take exactly the same approach when putting a menu together – think of the cocktail as an additional course. So I ask you to think about the drink you made for yourself to sip while you read. Are you enjoying it? Why or why not? What drove you to pick that drink – convenience, taste, nostalgia? Did a certain aroma or taste start to build and overpower? Make a note of your thoughts as we move along, remembering that there are no right or wrong answers; this is about you building an understanding of what a drink is, to you, in a given moment.

In Chapter 1, we laid a foundation for our view of cocktails. My aim in this chapter is to add a core structure: we are building an awareness of what needs to be considered to deliver delicious and enjoyable drinks. The knowledge you gain will help you to understand the potential of a cocktail so that the next time you read a recipe or look at a menu you will be able to envisage how that drink should taste and know more about what that experience may hold. You should also be able to start to apply this core structure approach to products and ingredients you use in drinks. This insight will help you to maximize your home bar, and ultimately, I hope you will be able to apply this thought process to 'non-traditional' ingredients you may have at hand. If you don't have any citrus, for example, you'll know what else could work and how to adjust your cocktail recipe to suit. We started by looking at the experience of food. Let's now delve deeper into each individual element involved in flavour and preference in the context of a cocktail.

OUR FOUNDATIONS

Whether or not this is something you have consciously paid attention to, your everyday consumption of food and drink will have exposed you to the five basic tastes, along with a multitude of different aromas. These experiences form our cocktail foundations. Below, I've suggested a few exercises you can do to build an awareness of the structure of the basic tastes, along with more specific details about how we experience aroma.

SWEET

We all want to reduce our sugar intake, but a little sugar in your drink goes a long way in helping create a balanced and pleasing cocktail. It assists in the perception of flavour, smooths out the sensation of alcohol on the palate and gives body to a cocktail. For these reasons, very few cocktails contain no sugar. If you are not adding it in the form of a sugar syrup, it will be there in a fruit juice, vermouth or liqueur. The recipes in this book that use sugar or sweet ingredients are balanced to give a universally likeable cocktail. I would suggest that you make the cocktails to recipe so that you first understand how the sugar is working. Then, if you personally feel the need to reduce or increase the sugar in a cocktail, do so gradually so that you may better judge the effect and retain as much balance as possible.

TASTE TEST

1   Brew 200ml (6⅔oz) of a standard black tea according to its brewing instructions
2   Divide the liquid into 2 heatproof glasses or cups.
3   Add 1 tsp of sugar to one glass only and stir to dissolve. Allow the liquids to cool to room temperature, or place in the refrigerator to chill.
4   Taste the sweetened and non-sweetened tea side by side and note how the taste, aroma, astringency and texture is different in the two teas.

SOUR

Sour as a taste is literally a mouth-watering experience. The reaction of sour on our palates causes us to salivate, preparing and cleansing our palates for taste and creating a 'mouth-watering' experience. Lemons and limes are the sour cocktail ingredient staples. Limes contain less sugar and are more acidic than lemons. While both have a bright aroma we would describe as citrus, lemons have a slight floral note and limes are a little spicier and greener in aroma.

As well as citrus, sour fruits can have a place in drinks along with vinegars and to some extent wines. These kitchen cupboard ingredients can be interesting to explore within their own right. It's important to remember that a sour ingredient will need to be balanced within a drink, and this is where sugar can come into play. We'll go into this in more detail when we explore the structure of sour cocktails (see page 151).

TASTE TEST
....

1   Take 3 glasses and pour 100ml (3⅓oz) of cold water into each glass.
2   Taking fresh juice that you have just squeezed, add 20ml (⅔oz) of lemon juice to the first glass, 20ml (⅔oz) of lime juice to the second glass and 20ml (⅔oz) of pink grapefruit juice to the third glass.
3   Note the aroma of each liquid.
4   Taste the liquids independently, paying attention to the difference in intensity of acid, sweetness and aroma.

BITTER

Bitter is an intense taste that takes time to break down on the palate, meaning this tastant will build and intensify as you consume it. Bitter liqueurs have become more mainstream as our palates have become more accustomed to and accepting of bitter tastes. However, these ingredients are quite specific, so they do not feature heavily in this book. If you know you love bitter, then I recommend you explore the world of amaro.

One ingredient every cocktail cabinet needs is cocktail bitters such as Angostura, as a dash of something bitter gives backbone to a drink. Angostura's concentrated taste and aroma make it the cocktail equivalent of Worcestershire sauce – in a sense it is the 'seasoning' for a cocktail and a little goes a long way. There is now a vast and exciting range of cocktail bitters easily available. From chocolate to grapefruit, bitters can be a great way to add a little flavour personalization to your drink. If this is something you'd like to explore, think about how robust or light your cocktail flavours are and try to complement this. Cocktail bitters have a long shelf life and are used in a wide range of drinks, so it is worth having a bottle of Angostura to hand at the least; you can even cook with them.

TASTE TEST

. . . .

1   Add a few dashes of any cocktail bitters you have, individually, to a glass of water.
2   Taste, thinking about what you perceive. The dilution will open up the bitters' flavour profile, making it easier for you to perceive the aroma. Dilution also makes the bitter taste less intense, making it easier to focus on the aroma.

SALT

Not the most common ingredient in a cocktail, but salt certainly has its place – there is nothing more pleasing than a salt rim on a Margarita. Saline solutions have been experimented with over recent years, the idea being that they brighten the flavour of a drink in a similar way to salt in our food. Salt also suppresses bitter taste receptors in the mouth, so when salt is added to a drink, we perceive any bitter tastes in a more subdued way. This is useful to know if you want to balance any overly bitter ingredients in your cocktail.

TASTE TEST
....

1   Brew a cup of black coffee or squeeze a glass of fresh grapefruit juice.
2   Dissolve 1 tsp of salt into 50ml (1⅔oz) of cold water to make a saline solution.
3   Taste your selected liquid, paying attention to its bitter taste.
4   Add a few drops of the saline solution and taste again, paying attention to how the intensity of bitter as a taste has changed.
5   Feel free to keep on adding drops of saline solution and tasting with this in mind.

UMAMI

Umami is the savoury taste we experience when eating ingredients such as tomatoes, mushrooms, soy sauce, miso and Parmesan cheese. The Bloody Mary (see page 204) is one of the most popular umami-rich cocktails. Umami can work as a basic taste bridge, linking ingredients to create a more pleasing experience. Try making yourself a Dirty Gin Martini (see page 107) as the simple addition of savoury olive brine brings a whole new experience to this cocktail. You'll also find umami in sherry, which can be fun to play with in drinks, especially Martinis.

TASTE TEST
....

1   Taste one of the ingredients listed above, focusing on the savoury taste as you consume it. That is umami.
2   Try adding soy sauce or miso to a tomato sauce to amplify the sauce's savoury quality. This will help to build your palate's understanding of what umami is.

ORTHONASAL OLFACTION

Orthonasal olfaction is the technical term for perceiving aroma through the nostrils when we sniff. It is a powerful experience we often tie to emotions, through memories –think about a loved one's favourite perfume. When we smell these familiar scents in other contexts, we relive the positive emotions tied to those memories. Scent can therefore be quite a nostalgic experience.

Alcohol, by its very nature, 'strips' and 'traps' aromatic molecules from other ingredients. Take gin as an example; its neutral alcohol base becomes the vehicle for a multilayered aromatic experience. Various botanicals are macerated in this base to extract their aromatic compounds. This maceration is then distilled to create the gin we know and love. Alcohol is also volatile; it wants to evaporate. This is useful to us, as any aromas trapped within the alcohol will evaporate along with it, aiding our orthonasal perception of aromas held within the liquid.

Additionally, a cocktail's glass funnels the aroma of the drink directly into our noses, giving us a sensory preview of what is to come when we consume the liquid. Cocktails can make a powerful impression via their aroma. This is a defining moment and aroma will make or break a drink. Do not underestimate the power of scent when it comes to cocktails – a pleasant aroma will make you want to sip, but anything 'off' and you'll put the drink down without even trying it. A cocktail's aroma does not need to be complex, but you must ensure there is nothing off-putting there. Be conscious of egg white in this respect, as this is an ingredients that will give a slight 'wet dog' aroma on the nose.

AWARENESS TEST
....

Consciously smell every ingredient before you work with it; pay attention to what you notice so that you start to build a library of aroma in your mind.

To understand how alcohol strips aroma, try this test.

1   Pour 100ml (3⅓oz) of vodka into a wine glass and add 2g (1 tsp) of aromatic tea such as green tea or jasmine tea.

2   Cover the glass and leave to infuse for 5 minutes.

3   Uncover the glass and smell the liquid, paying attention to what you perceive. You may want to swill the glass as you would wine to release more aromatic compounds into the headspace (the space that's directly above the surface of the liquid).

4   Cover the glass again and leave to infuse for a further 5 minutes. Repeat the process, noting how the aromas develop.

You make also like to taste the liquid as you go, paying attention to the aromas you perceive along the way.

RETRONASAL OLFACTION

Retronasal aroma is a very different experience to orthonasal, as it does not happen in isolation – we are also experiencing tastants, via our taste buds, at the same time. When we take a sip of a drink, we hold that liquid in our mouths for a few moments and then swallow. During this process, not only do we taste the liquid and experience any chemesthetic qualities it holds, but aroma molecules are released and travel up through our retronasal passage to the roof of the nasal cavity. Here, they interact with our olfactory epithelium, soft tissue that holds olfactory receptors. This is the start of our olfactory system, the sensory system by which we perceive smell. Think of retronasal as the 'back door' entrance for aroma. It's vital to our enjoyment of food and drink.

The release of aromatic compounds is influenced by how we consume a drink. When we move a liquid around our mouths, we stimulate the release of aroma molecules. As cold liquids warm on the palate, the release of aromatic molecules increases. However, we often swallow so quickly that we reduce our exposure to the aroma held within a liquid. We don't have to chew a drink in order to swallow it, and because of this, we perhaps don't spend the time thinking about our retronasal aroma experience of a liquid in the same way as we do food. Be conscious of how you consume a drink: sometimes taking the time to be aware of what it is you are experiencing is all that is needed to change how you understand and value it.

AWARENESS TEST

Consciously smell then taste an ingredient, thinking about how its aroma evolves and is linked to its overall flavour. This can be done with the orthonasal tea vodka test opposite.

For a clear retronasal experience, try this test.

1   With your fingers, pinch your nose closed.
2   Put a jelly bean or sweet in your mouth. Can you taste anything? Can you perceive any aroma or fruity flavours?
3   Release your fingers from your nose, allowing the aromas to pass up through your retronasal passages. What can you perceive now? On releasing your fingers, you should have had a very clear hit of aroma and now be able to experience the full flavour of your sweet.

THE PHYSICAL CORE OF A COCKTAIL

Our core structure is made up of the physical traits of a cocktail. An awareness of these elements will help in building your understanding of what flavour is how it makes a great drink.

ALCOHOL CONTENT

Alcohol gives a chemesthetic sensation of heat on the palate; the higher the ABV (alcohol by volume) of a product or cocktail, the stronger the 'burn' will be. Most alcoholic products are designed to be mixed with other complementary spirits, diluted or served over ice. This means that the sensation of heat on the palate is reduced and made more pleasant. It's also possible to build a tolerance to ABV. Through repeated exposure, the palate can become desensitized to the burn sensation. Refer to the section on Stirred Cocktails (see page 99) for more details.

There are two alcohol-related elements that can influence your enjoyment of a cocktail. The first is your choice of alcohol in a cocktail and the expected ABV of the finished drink. Sometimes we enjoy the sensation of alcohol on the palate and sometimes we do not. When planning and making a cocktail, think about the strength of alcohol in the final drink and make sure it is appropriate for the mood and the occasion. The second element to consider is how well the cocktail has been made, which is where dilution comes in.

DILUTION

Nearly all cocktails need water. Dilution is added by stirring or shaking with ice – as the ice cools the liquid, it melts, adding water to the cocktail. A cocktail can also be diluted by topping up with a mixer such as soda or tonic water. The only cocktails that do not need water are the lower-ABV drinks that tend to use ingredients such as Champagne or Prosecco, which themselves act as the dilution for any stronger ingredients used in the cocktail.

Dilution softens tastants and assists in the perception of aroma by opening up the profile of the liquid. Think of how fruit cordials work; they taste sweet and flat in their undiluted form, but when mixed in a glass of water we perceive a more balanced sweetness, a little sourness and a fruity aroma. Dilution will also affect the texture of a drink, making it seem thin and watery on the palate if over-diluted or thick and closed if under-diluted. Always use the best-quality ice when making and serving your drinks, as it will lower the temperature of your cocktails without over-diluting them. If you use lower-quality ice, pay great attention, as it is very easy to over-dilute a cocktail with it.

It's a matter of finding the perfect level where the sensation of alcohol is correct, basic tastes are balanced and aromas have opened up. Don't overlook the method when making a cocktail – pay attention to your liquid while making to ensure you achieve the desired results. And keep making and tasting – at some point you will develop the intuition to find the dilution sweet spot.

DILUTION AWARENESS TEST

1. Prepare 3 Dry Gin Martinis (see page 104), stirring the first Martini 5 times, the second Martini 10 times and the third Martini 20 times.
2. Place each drink in the fridge for 10 minutes to standardize their temperatures.
3. Taste each Martini. Take note of the difference in sensation of alcohol and how the tastes and flavours change between the three drinks.

TEMPERATURE

To understand the importance of temperature in a cocktail, I'd like to ask you to pick your favourite Martini you've just made in the dilution test above. You'll have just sipped it a few times at its optimum temperature straight from the fridge. Now leave that Martini at room temperature for 10 minutes. The liquid should now be warmer – go ahead and taste the drink. How does it compare? A warm Martini is an undrinkable Martini.

Temperature affects the perception of alcohol and astringency of a cocktail, with a cold drink being more palatable. It will also change how you perceive sweetness; a drink will taste sweeter as it warms. Make sure your cocktail is chilled correctly, that any mixers are chilled and, where required, glasses are chilled. This will make a huge impact on the quality of your drinks.

ASTRINGENCY

Astringency is the drying sensation we feel on our tongues when we consume certain wines and teas, and it comes from the presence of tannins. Tannins are also found in oak and can be perceived in darker spirits that have been aged in oak barrels. They are useful, as they can help cut through intense taste and assist, in a similar way cocktail bitters do, in the creation of a 'backbone' in a cocktail. They give us a structure on which we can pin other ingredients.

TEXTURE

As a cocktail is one whole liquid consumed from one glass, the texture of that liquid needs to please. Think about the fine bubbles in a Champagne cocktail or the refreshing fizz from a Collins that contains soda water – these are both pleasing textural experiences. Add sugar to a cocktail and you will add a subtle and pleasing silky smooth texture. I personally love a sour for its texture more than its taste. It's my go-to drink when I'm unsure what I want, as I know the texture of the foamy egg white on the palate always pleases me.

Fat can also have a place in drinks in the form of the almond-based syrup orgeat, milk or cream, and in fat washing. This technique involves mixing a spirit with an ingredient such as melted butter or cream and then freezing it so that the fat solidifies and can be strained out of the liquid. The resulting alcohol has the flavour of the fat without containing the fat itself, allowing us to give an impression of texture without creating heavy, fat-based drinks.

THE PIVOT POINT OF PREFERENCE

This section is about looking at the foundation and core structures from different perspectives, then picking the right route forward to create an enjoyable experience. The following headings are the pivot points that may lead your preferences in specific or different directions, and much of this is influenced by the occasion. There are two key sides to consider here – your preferences and those of your guests. Our personal preference is driven by flavour but influenced by memories, emotions and desires. You may have a core preference that never changes; this will probably be based on tastes such as a liking for sweet drinks and a dislike of strong bitter drinks. However, our preferences tend to change with our mood and the moment in time. Think about what you like to drink on a warm sunny day and compare it to a wintery festive occasion – you may choose a sweet drink on both occasions, but the overall flavour experience you choose to consume will likely be different.

I ask that for the final section of this chapter you take your own personal preferences into account. Once you have applied these concepts to your preferences, you should be able to take what you learn and apply it to your guests' point of view.

ENVIRONMENT, TIME AND LOGISTICS OF SERVICE

The time, location and mood can influence your cocktail preference, especially when it comes to alcohol content and intensity of flavour. Think about how these three elements influence your cocktail choices.

If you're hosting, take into account the time of day and the food you might be serving. This will give you a lead in selecting cocktails of an appropriate alcohol content and accessible flavour direction. Never forget the test of a great drink – can you finish it, and when you do, would you like to order exactly the same again? If the answer's yes, your intensity and balance are correct. If you keep cocktails simple and accessible, you'll find hosting the most rewarding experience.

COMMITTING TO AN EXPERIENCE

If you're hosting, your drinks must suit a universal palate. The key when it comes to keeping guests happy is to be humble, honest and realistic. We all want to share our favourite taste and flavour experiences, but we aren't all the same. Subtlety, simplicity and a little variety can go a long way with guests. The good news is that if your drinks have an approachable flavour and balanced structure, they will generally please everyone.

KEEP IT SIMPLE

Take into account the logistics of making cocktails, especially when hosting. What's realistic for you to serve quickly and consistently? The goal is to minimize the stress of making cocktails for guests, meaning you all have more fun together. So curate your cocktail menus wisely – often less is more.

2
THE COCKTAILS

CHAPTER 6: CHAMPAGNE COCKTAILS

Champagne cocktails offer a good starting point to work practically with our foundation and core principles. This is because the focus of a Champagne cocktail is, not surprisingly, the Champagne itself. Champagne provides a structure we can hang all of our other cocktail ingredients off, so let's look into this in more detail.

For me, Champagne has always been a luxury; the sensation of fine bubbles held within this liquid is unlike anything else. It's a pure indulgence. Champagne is not something I always have to hand at home, so when I do reach for it, I know that what is to come will be a moment of ritual that signifies celebration. This association makes Champagne a liquid that taps into our emotions. It's the ceremonial act of the pop of a bottle that gives a rush of excitement, a key factor in the success of Champagne cocktails. Essentially, with this category of cocktails, we are looking to build on this moment of anticipation to create something extra special. As a host, the time and effort you put into making these cocktails creates a personalized approach to celebration. So enjoy making these drinks, as in the process, you'll be creating some unforgettable moments that I'm sure your guests will appreciate.

KEEP IT SIMPLE

We need to embrace the fact that this is a liquid that imparts a positive mood before we've even started. Therefore, to make a successful Champagne cocktail, it's vital you keep it simple; let the beauty of this ingredient and the ritual of its experience shine through. Champagne cocktails need to lead with the qualities of their key ingredient: Champagne. This is of benefit to us, as it simplifies the structure of these cocktails, making them approachable and adaptable. This means we can play and personalize with ease. For these drinks to taste great we need to:

1   Keep the balance between sweet and sour tastes.
2   Take a 'less is more' approach to the intensity of aroma that's added to
    the Champagne.
3   Keep the bubbles intact so that we still experience the amazing texture
    of Champagne.

Think of making these cocktails as upgrading the Champagne. The Champagne will stay true to itself and be recognizable, but at the same time the cocktail will present a different experience. It's rather like toast and jam, with the toast being the Champagne. Toast and jam go hand in hand, but jam is too concentrated and intense on its own; it needs to be served with another ingredient so that its flavour profile opens up. And while bread is a pleasure in itself, especially when its savoury and yeasty aromas are amplified through toasting, it is also versatile. Its balanced flavour profile makes it delicious on its own, yet it is also compatible with a wide range of other ingredients – be it something that is sweet, sour or savoury. Toast has the added bonus of giving a physical structure to work with; it becomes the vessel to deliver the flavour experience we desire. To make a tasty snack, all we need are two ingredients prepared in a way that they harmonize with each other. This is also the case with the Kir Royale, a cocktail made from a measure of a fruit-based crème liqueur (our jam) topped with Champagne (our toast), and the first recipe in this category of cocktails (see page 82).

Keep the harmony of toast and jam in mind and you'll find that Champagne cocktails are amazing vessels you can use to explore a range of flavours. Think about the flavours you enjoy and utilize ingredients you already have in your spirit collection – gin, Cognac, rum and liqueurs all have a place here.

BE MINDFUL OF THE BUBBLES

The goal is to preserve as much of the fizz as possible. Using a jigger will destroy the bubbles within the liquid, so it's best to top up your Champagne cocktails straight from the bottle into the serving glass. However, you will need to add the correct amount of Champagne to ensure the drink is balanced. To achieve this, we're going to make a wash-line visual aid so you know how much Champagne to add. Over time, or if you have a confident eye, you may find that you can memorize the wash-lines for these cocktails and not need to follow the steps below every time.

1   Take a spare glass, the same type you will use for your selected cocktail.
2   Refer to the total volume of your cocktail in the recipe. Add this volume of water to your spare glass.
3   Keep this visual aid at your bar station, close to where you will make the cocktails.
4   When you come to make your cocktails, top them up with Champagne until you reach the same wash-line as the water in the spare glass.

If you don't have a spare glass to do this, you can still use a jigger to measure the Champagne in the traditional way, but just take it slow and be very gentle when pouring.

Finally, when it comes to stirring Champagne cocktails, do this very gently. Normally one stir is enough to combine the ingredients, passing the spoon in a full 360-degree motion while gently pulling the spoon up through the liquid.

INGREDIENTS FOR CHAMPAGNE COCKTAILS

FROM YOUR DRINKS CABINET

Brut Champagne

Absinthe

Angostura bitters

Cognac

Crème liqueurs – cassis and apricot are useful,
      but most fruit liqueurs will work

Guinness or stout beer

Light aged rum

London dry gin

Mezcal espadin

Oloroso sherry

Vodka

ADDITIONAL ITEMS

Elderflower cordial

Fresh lemons

Fresh limes

Fresh oranges

Fresh orange juice without pulp (squeezed or shop bought)

Honey – a neutral, lightly flavoured honey is best

Sugar syrup

White sugar cubes

KIR ROYALE

15ml (½oz) crème de cassis

115ml (3⅔oz plus 1 tsp)
  Champagne

Total drink volume: 130ml (4⅓oz)

Ideal glass volume: 165–285ml
  (5½–9½oz)

Glass: Champagne flute or tulip at
  room temperature

The Kir Royale is our starting point, as it's the simplest of the Champagne cocktails, and while there is a notable change in flavour from the addition of the crème liqueur, the Champagne still shines through. By using only one additional ingredient, we are bringing alcohol, sweetness, acidity and aroma to a glass of Champagne. The Kir Royale, in essence, becomes a learning tool to help us understand how flavour interacts with and changes Champagne. This creates a reference point for all of the drinks in this category.

So that you can perceive how different fruit flavours work with the flavour of Champagne, I recommend trying this recipe with a few different crème liqueurs. This will help to build your palate knowledge and aid in the understanding of your personal preferences. Feel free to experiment – if you believe the flavours will work with Champagne, go ahead and try it.

Add the crème de cassis to the glass and top up with the Champagne. Using a bar spoon, gently stir the liquid to combine, then serve.

Note: Crème liqueur brands will differ in intensity of flavour. My recommendation is to make one cocktail in advance to test the balance of tastes. You should be able to perceive the fruit flavours, but the drink should not be overly sweet. I also advise doing this if you are switching to a different fruit liqueur. For example, I like cassis at 15ml (½oz), but prefer peach crème liqueur at 10ml (2 tsp). Note that if you reduce the liqueur volume, you will be increasing the Champagne volume if you maintain the same wash-line, so make small adjustments, as they can have a greater impact than expected.

CRÈME DE CASSIS

CHAMPAGNE

DEATH IN THE AFTERNOON

5ml (1 tsp) absinthe

2.5ml (½ tsp) Sugar Syrup
(see page 59)

115ml (3⅔oz plus 1 tsp)
Champagne

Total drink volume: 122.5ml
(4oz plus ½ tsp)

Ideal glass volume: 165–285ml
(5½–9½oz)

Glass: coupette at room
temperature

*This drink won't be for everyone, but if you enjoy aniseed and herbal
green flavours, I suggest you try this cocktail. The absinthe works great
with Champagne.*

*Traditional recipes for Death in the Afternoon have a much higher
proportion of absinthe than mine. I have to admit that when testing those
recipes, I found the cocktails very hard to drink, let alone finish. So my version
is balanced so that the absinthe flavours are present, but do not overshadow
the Champagne.*

*Absinthe is intense in flavour: it has a very high ABV, contains no sugar
and has a slight bitter note. If our aim is to keep the balance of this drink
similar to that of a Kir Royale, then we need to add a touch of sugar to smooth
off the alcohol, help the flavours integrate and ultimately balance the cocktail.*

Add the absinthe and sugar syrup to the glass and top up with the
Champagne. Using a bar spoon, gently stir the liquid to combine,
then serve.

Note: If you'd like this cocktail to have more of an absinthe kick, then do
increase its volume. I suggest that you start with 2.5ml (½ tsp) increases and
pay attention to the sugar, as you'll probably need to increase that too.

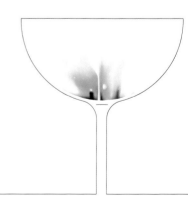

ABSINTHE

SUGAR SYRUP

CHAMPAGNE

BLACK VELVET

70ml (2⅓oz) Guinness

70ml (2⅓oz) Champagne

Total drink volume: 140ml (4⅔oz)

Ideal glass volume: 165–285ml

(5½–9½oz)

Glass: Champagne flute at room

temperature

Building on the relationship and balance of two elements, the ingredients in this cocktail harmonize to produce a rich and warming Champagne cocktail that verges on the savoury side. The roasted malt notes and slightly bitter-sweet taste of the Guinness work incredibly well with the biscuity aroma profile of the Champagne. There is no need to add sugar to this drink – the Guinness gives us enough sweetness to work well with the Champagne.

Although the Champagne is not the leading flavour in this drink, what makes this cocktail unique is the textural experience. Both ingredients have a unique texture that, when combined, produce something like the sensation of velvet on the palate.

Add the Guinness to the glass and slowly top with the Champagne. Using a bar spoon, very gently stir to combine, then serve.

Note: The recipe uses the same quantity of each ingredient, so if your glass is larger or smaller than that suggested, you can easily scale it up or down to suit your needs.

Feel free to try this drink with your favourite stout and explore how the flavours change. Equally, if the flavour of Guinness or stout is too strong for you, reduce the volume of this ingredient and increase the volume of the Champagne in the cocktail. If you find this cocktail a little bitter, feel free to add a touch of sugar syrup: start with 1.25ml (¼ tsp) and increase to suit your taste.

■ GUINNESS

□ CHAMPAGNE

From left to right: Death in the Afternoon (see page 84) and Black Velvet (see page 85)

SMOKY ROYALE

5ml (1 tsp) mezcal espadin

10ml (2 tsp) apricot liqueur

115ml (3⅔oz plus 1 tsp)
  Champagne

Total drink volume: 130ml (4⅓oz)

Ideal glass volume: 165–285ml
  (5½–9½oz)

Glass: Champagne flute at room
  temperature

The structure of this cocktail sits between the Kir Royale (see page 82) and Death in the Afternoon (see page 84), so keep the principles from those two cocktails in mind here. The warm, stone fruit aroma of the apricot liqueur sits well with the smokiness of the mezcal and brings a sweetness to the drink that is not dissimilar to that of the Kir Royale.

Add the mezcal espadin and apricot liqueur to the glass and top up with the Champagne. Using a bar spoon, gently stir the liquid to combine, then serve.

Note: Mezcal has a distinct flavour profile that will easily overpower other flavours. A light touch here with this product ensures we keep an overall balance of flavour. Bear this in mind if you do wish to experiment with different types of mezcal.

MEZCAL ESPADIN

APRICOT LIQUEUR

CHAMPAGNE

TWINKLE

25ml (⅔oz plus 1t sp) vodka
15ml (½oz) elderflower cordial
100ml (3⅓oz) Champagne
long lemon peel

Total drink volume: approximately
    150ml (5oz)
Ideal glass volume: 165–285ml
    (5½–9½oz)
Glass: large coupette glass

Invented in a small yet iconic neighbourhood bar, The Bar with No Name in London, this drink is said to put a twinkle in your eye. The Twinkle is a contemporary Champagne cocktail that has achieved cult status – you will see this cocktail on menus all over the world, demonstrating how well-balanced drinks create classic cocktails. While the vodka provides a Champagne cocktail experience with a little more alcoholic kick, the elderflower cordial bridges the space between the vodka and the Champagne, creating a drink that is aromatic, smooth and fun.

Fill a cocktail shaker with cubed ice. Add the vodka and elderflower cordial, seal the shaker and hard shake. Double strain the liquid into the glass and top up with the Champagne. Garnish with a long lemon peel that's had its oils expressed over surface of the liquid and serve.

VODKA

ELDERFLOWER CORDIAL

CHAMPAGNE

CHAMPAGNE COCKTAIL

1 white sugar cube
6 dashes of Angostura bitters
15ml (½oz) Cognac
100ml (3⅓oz) Champagne

Total drink volume: 115ml
   (3⅔oz plus 1 tsp)
Ideal glass volume: 150–240ml
   (5–8oz plus 1 tsp)
Glass: coupette at room
   temperature

This is an iconic cocktail with great depth of flavour, yet it remains approachable to guests. Though a little stronger in spirit, we've retained balance with the warm flavour profile of all the ingredients involved. The spices from the Angostura bitters complement the Cognac's woody profile and act as a bridge between the Cognac and Champagne. This is a richer, deeper-flavoured cocktail, especially when compared with the bright fruity notes of the Kir Royale (see page 82).

What's great about this drink is that the aroma delivery system has changed and this is because of the sugar cube. The sugar cube encourages and becomes the starting point for the bubbles, and this is important. Each bubble carries with it the aroma of the bitters, making this cocktail a great example of the impact aroma has on the drinking experience. It's therefore important you stick with a sugar cube – sugar syrup would taste fine, but the aroma of the drink will be reduced.

Place the sugar cube on a napkin and dash the bitters on to the sugar cube; it should be fully covered in the bitters. Place the soaked sugar cube in the glass, add the Cognac and top up with the Champagne, then serve.

Note: You do not stir this cocktail, as you do not want to disturb the sugar cube. The goal is to let it gently release the flavour from the bitters while it slowly dissolves and makes the cocktail sweeter. The drink will therefore get sweeter as it sits, so don't be concerned if this cocktail is dry at the start. Enjoy the experience of it changing over time.

WHITE SUGAR CUBE

ANGOSTURA BITTERS

COGNAC

CHAMPAGNE

SHERRY CHAMPAGNE COCKTAIL

1 white sugar cube

6 dashes of Angostura bitters

15ml (½oz) oloroso sherry

100ml (3⅔oz) Champagne

Total drink volume: 115ml
(3⅔oz plus 1 tsp)

Ideal glass volume: 150–240ml
(5–8oz plus 1 tsp)

Glass: coupette at room
temperature

*A twist on the Champagne Cocktail (see page 90), this drink pushes
Champagne into a more savoury space. Oloroso is a rich and fragrant sherry
that will give us enough of a structure to work with in this cocktail.*

Place the sugar cube on a napkin and dash the bitters on to the sugar cube;
it should be fully covered in the bitters. Place the soaked sugar cube in the
glass, add the sherry and top up with the Champagne, then serve.

Note: If you enjoy this cocktail, it is worth exploring the different styles
of dry sherries available. The range of savoury and mineral flavour profiles
you can work with here is vast. Pay attention to how the bitters work in
this cocktail – you may wish to vary the quantity if they start to overpower
the cocktail.

WHITE SUGAR CUBE

ANGOSTURA BITTERS

OLOROSO SHERRY

CHAMPAGNE

MIMOSA

70ml (2⅓oz) fresh orange juice without pulp
70ml (2⅓oz) Champagne

Total drink volume: 140ml (4⅔oz)
Ideal glass volume: 165–285ml (5½–9½oz)
Glass: Champagne flute at room temperature

This is our first Champagne cocktail with the addition of citrus, taking this drink into a slightly different space, as the higher acid content changes the impact of the Champagne. That is not to say the Mimosa is anything but a great drink, it just means that we are moving into a new flavour direction.

Here, we revisit the relationship of two ingredients to create what is classically seen as a morning celebration cocktail. Its lower ABV and breakfast orange juice association makes this cocktail very approachable. This drink should be fresh yet indulgent.

If your fresh orange juice contains pulp, first strain it through a fine sieve. Add the fresh orange juice to the glass and slowly top up with the Champagne. Using a bar spoon, very gently stir to combine, then serve.

Note: Ideally, your orange juice should have enough natural sugar to balance the taste of this cocktail. However, oranges vary from season to season and orange juice will vary from brand to brand. If the finished cocktail tastes overly sour, do consider adding a touch of sugar syrup. I recommend starting at 1.25ml (¼ tsp), tasting and increasing if you feel the need.

Note that there are equal quantities of the two ingredients, so if your glass is larger or smaller than that suggested, you can easily scale the recipe up or down to suit your needs. Also, if you increase the proportion of Champagne to orange juice, this cocktail becomes a Bucks Fizz.

FRESH ORANGE JUICE

CHAMPAGNE

FRENCH 75

30ml (1oz) citrus-led gin, such as
    Beefeater, or Cognac
20ml (⅔oz) fresh lemon juice
10ml (2 tsp) Sugar Syrup
    (see age 59)
65ml (2oz plus 1 tsp) Champagne
twist of lemon peel

Total drink volume: 125ml
    (4oz plus 1 tsp)
Ideal glass volume: 165–285ml
    (5½–9½oz)
Glass: tulip or small highball at
    room temperature

There are two versions of the French 75 – one with gin and one with Cognac. It may sound a little surprising to add gin to Champagne, but think about how well gin pairs with citrus and you can hopefully build a picture in your mind of how this cocktail will taste. If anything, the ability to switch between gin and Cognac demonstrates just how versatile Champagne is.

The French 75 is our first Champagne cocktail that is shaken. As we are adding more alcohol and acid, we require a touch of dilution, which we do by shaking. In case you wonder, the Champagne itself is never shaken, as this would destroy the bubbles and possibly cause your cocktail shaker to explode!

Fill a cocktail shaker with cubed ice. Add your chosen spirit, fresh lemon juice and sugar syrup. Seal the shaker and hard shake. Double strain the liquid into the glass and top up with the Champagne. Using a bar spoon, gently stir the liquid to combine. Garnish with a lemon peel twist and serve.

Note: My suggestion is to start with a classic citrus-led gin here, as it will complement the lemon juice and create a focused flavour profile for the finished cocktail. You'll also gain an understanding of how traditional gin works as a product. A more complex flavour profile can be built with the use of contemporary gins. Ultimately, this will be your choice, and my advice is to look at the key ingredients in your selected gin and think about how they will pair with the flavour of Champagne. As always, test a change before serving to a guest and look out for any flavours that 'peak up' and throw off the balance of the cocktail.

CITRUS-LED GIN

TWIST OF LEMON PEEL

SUGAR SYRUP

CHAMPAGNE

AIRMAIL

30ml (1oz) light aged rum, such as Havana Club 3 Años

20ml (⅔oz) fresh lime juice

10ml (2 tsp) Honey Syrup (see below)

65ml (2oz plus 1 tsp) Champagne

discarded orange disc

a single shard of ice or several cubes, to serve

Total drink volume: 125ml (4oz plus 1 tsp)

Ideal glass volume: 165–285ml (5½–9½oz)

Glass: small highball at room temperature

I encourage you to try this one! To me, this cocktail's flavour fills the gap between a gin French 75 and a Cognac French 75 (see page 95). Plus, it's a fun drink that is often overlooked. You'll notice that an Airmail has the exact same structure as a French 75 in terms of the proportion of alcohol, acid, sugar and Champagne. But there are switches in ingredients and this is led by the change to a light aged rum. Both lime and honey complement the fresh, citrus and slightly nutty, woody notes of the rum – rum and lime is a pairing often found in classic Cuban cocktails. The warm citrus aroma from a discarded orange disc brings all of the ingredients together. The overall effect is an alluring cocktail worth exploring.

Fill a cocktail shaker with cubed ice. Add the rum, fresh lime juice and honey syrup. Seal the shaker and hard shake. Double strain the liquid into a glass containing a shard of ice and top up with the Champagne. Using a bar spoon, gently stir the liquid to combine. Express the oils from the orange disc over the surface of the liquid, discard it and serve.

Note: The flavour profile of different honeys varies – for example, you'll find sweet floral notes in orange blossom honey and warm nutty notes in chestnut honey. If you'd like to explore this drink in more detail, I suggest you first try a selection of different honeys and see how that affects the flavour profile of the cocktail.

Honey syrup: First calculate how much honey syrup you need by looking at how many cocktails you'd like to make. In a measuring jug, combine two parts of a light floral honey with one part of warm water. Stir the mixture until the honey has dissolved into the water. This can be done in advance and stored in your bar station.

WHITE SUGAR CUBE

ANGOSTURA BITTERS

OLOROSO SHERRY

CHAMPAGNE

CHAPTER 7:
STIRRED COCKTAILS

Unlike Champagne cocktails, the focus of this chapter is not an ingredient but the method of making: stirring. While I was thinking about how to present the different cocktail categories, it occurred to me that stirring is a defining process that consistently results in shorter cocktails of a higher alcohol content. This gives us a consistent core consideration to work with across the spirit groups within this cocktail category, and we will explore the different spirits individually.

The structure of a stirred cocktail focuses on the drink's main spirit, pushing its flavour profile towards a new experience through the addition of other ingredients. But as the spirit takes centre stage, so too does the alcohol content. It's not uncommon for stirred cocktails to have a stronger physical sensation or 'burn' on the palate and that can take some getting used to. The iconic Martini, made from gin and dry vermouth, is a classic example of this impactful style of cocktail.

My first Martini was an experience I had to force a smile through. My palate was just not accustomed to the alcohol burn sensation, and the lack of sweetness and acid made me feel like I was drinking pure gin. I persevered (a consequence of working in a cocktail bar where the in-house Martini was iconic), and eventually came to love the ritual of a Martini on a Friday night. Through this process, I learned a lot about my personal preference and it changed my approach to choosing and consuming cocktails; it was a key pivot point for me that I will share with you.

ADAPTATION

After a busy working week, every Friday night my colleagues and I would cheers each other and share a moment over gin, dry vermouth and an olive. Looking back, I'm unsure as to why no other drink was on offer, but it made me persevere with the Martini. After a few weeks I noticed the initial burn sensation was not so strong. What actually happened is that over time my palate adapted to the physical sensation of alcohol, making the burn seem less aggressive. Alcohol isn't the only thing our palates will adapt to – the same effect often happens with bitter tastes and sometimes with food we don't like. Through repeated exposure, we become less sensitive to these tastes and sensations. It then becomes a question of mind over matter and if we can start to like these drinks and foods. As Martinis became a ritual with colleagues and friends, it was easy for me to convert this experience into a pleasurable one.

TIME, TEMPERATURE AND QUALITY OVER QUANTITY

The biggest mistake I made with my first Martini was to consume it very slowly; it got warm and was undrinkable. Don't eek out a stirred cocktail to try to make the drink last, as the cold temperature of these drinks is vital to their enjoyment.

Take note that it's hard to keep a large volume of liquid chilled in a glass for the time it takes to drink it. Personally, I'd rather take the less-is-more approach and enjoy a smaller drink consumed at the perfect temperature than have one large drink I cannot finish because it's got warm. Therefore, the recipes in this book produce stirred cocktails that are normally less than 100ml (3⅓oz) in volume. The drinks are designed to be consumed within a time frame that allows them to stay cool in the glass. If a recipe asks you to chill a glass, do. This will help prolong the chill on the liquid and give the impression of a smoother cocktail.

DILUTION

Don't overlook the importance of dilution. Going back to my Friday-night Martinis, despite the bar team using exactly the same recipe, ingredients and equipment, one bartender somehow made the best Martinis. They had a sixth sense for when gin and dry vermouth were in their sweet spot – perfectly diluted, chilled, balanced and silky smooth. The correct amount of water added to a cocktail via ice dilution can make or break a drink. When stirring a cocktail, you're aiming to add enough water that the individual ingredients integrate and become one. This dilution opens up the flavour profile of the ingredients, making them more perceivable and enjoyable.

Dilution is a balancing act and something you can only learn through the practice of making and tasting cocktails. There have been many times when I've been developing cocktails with bar teams and there has been a desire to add more of an ingredient to make it taste stronger, when in actual fact, the cocktail just needed a little more dilution to bring out the flavour. Taste all of your cocktails before you strain and serve them, just as a bartender would. This will teach your palate the role dilution plays and provide you with the opportunity to add more dilution if needed.

Over-dilution is a different sensation; the liquid will lose its length of flavour. It's as if it is faint or in the distance and dissolving away. The texture of the drink will also be affected. It'll feel thin rather than smooth. Unfortunately, there is no fix for over-dilution; you will need to start the cocktail again from scratch.

Some stirred cocktails are served over ice. Generally, these cocktails require more chill over a longer period and can stand up to a little more dilution. There's an element of enjoyment to be had from the evolution of flavours opening up as the cocktail dilutes in the glass. As always, use good-quality ice to keep the liquid chilled and impart slow dilution to the drink. Poor-quality ice will melt quickly and your cocktail will over-dilute before you can finish it.

TASTANTS AND AROMATICS TO HELP US THROUGH

Sticking with the Martini, I learned my flavour preferences through trying different gins, vodkas and garnishes in these drinks, as well as experimenting with different styles of Martini (dry, wet, dirty, see pages 104–107). Learning your preferences takes time and comes down to a willingness to try new things, which can be a bit of a gigantic task. For now, I'd like to focus your attention on two elements of stirred cocktails – sweetness and the effect of the garnish. These two principles affect all stirred cocktails and may help you understand why you did or did not like a specific drink.

Sugar has had a hard time over recent years. And while we should all be conscious of how much we consume, it is an important ingredient in cocktails. Even a Martini has a touch of sugar in it – dry vermouth contains sugar. Sugar will soften the edge of the taste and feeling of alcohol on the palate. While I was allowing for my palate to adjust to the experience of strong cocktails, my go-to cocktail was a Martinez (see page 115), a cousin of the Martini. Made from gin, sweet vermouth, Boker's bitters and maraschino liqueur, it presented a more accessible route into drinking stronger cocktails. The switch to a richer flavour profile of sweet vermouth and a fruity liqueur, plus the addition of Boker's bitters with their warmer aroma and bitterness, softened the whole experience. So if you are new to this category of cocktails, you may wish to start with a cocktail recipe that has a slightly sweeter taste, as well as ingredients with familiar flavours you know you like; I'm a huge cherry fan.

The garnish is the last touch to a cocktail. A garnish should bring an aromatic element to emphasize or bring together the flavour profile of a cocktail. Going back to our iconic Martini, there are three traditional options: a lemon disc or twist with its oils expressed over the surface of the drink, an olive with its salty umami taste and fatty texture or a silver skin pickled cocktail onion (a Martini served with a small pickled onion is a Gibson cocktail, see page 108). Comparing these three garnish options, you'll notice that only two have tastants – the lemon peel has a purely aromatic function. What's interesting about this is that we can take the exact same cocktail liquid and change how it tastes through the addition of a garnish. I still find it hard to drink a Martini with a lemon disc. To me, the citrus gives a sharp edge to the drink, making it a touch too harsh for my palate. The creamy, salty taste a green olive imparts to the liquid is more where I'm at. I feel it pulls the liquid together, making it taste smoother, plus it's a little edible treat at the end of the drink. Pay attention to the details – garnishes have a function and more impact than you may think, so use this to your advantage.

INGREDIENTS FOR STIRRED COCKTAILS

GIN STIRRED COCKTAILS

FROM YOUR DRINKS CABINET

Gin – Beefeater and
    Sipsmith provide two
    useful flavour profiles
Dry vermouth
Sweet vermouth
Maraschino liqueur
Boker's bitters

ADDITIONAL ITEMS

Fresh lemons
Fresh limes
Fresh oranges
Green olives in brine
Lime cordial
Silver skin pickled cocktail onions

VODKA STIRRED COCKTAILS

FROM YOUR DRINKS CABINET

Vodka – ideally a smooth and
    creamy rye or wheat vodka
Dry vermouth
Fino sherry
Grapefruit bitters

ADDITIONAL ITEMS

Fresh lemons
Fresh pink grapefruits
Green olives in brine
Sugar Syrup (see page 59)

WHISKY AND COGNAC STIRRED COCKTAILS

FROM YOUR DRINKS CABINET
. . . .

Bourbon

Rye whiskey

Scotch whisky

Angostura bitters

Cognac

Dry vermouth

Maraschino liqueur

Pernod absinthe

Peychaud's bitters

Sweet vermouth

ADDITIONAL ITEMS
. . . .

Fresh lemons

Fresh oranges

Maraschino cherries

Sugar Syrup (see page 59)

RUM STIRRED COCKTAILS

FROM YOUR DRINKS CABINET
. . . .

Aged golden rum

Angostura bitters

Maraschino liqueur

Orange bitters

Sweet vermouth

Triple sec

ADDITIONAL ITEMS
. . . .

Fresh oranges

Grenadine (see page 59)

Maraschino cherries

Sugar Syrup (see page 59)

AGAVE STIRRED COCKTAILS

FROM YOUR DRINKS CABINET
. . . .

Mezcal espadin

Tequila reposado

Grapefruit bitters

Orange bitters

ADDITIONAL ITEMS
. . . .

Agave Syrup (see page 59)

Fresh grapefruits

Fresh oranges

DRY GIN MARTINI

50ml (1⅔oz) gin
10ml (2 tsp) dry vermouth
disc or twist of lemon peel
 or green olive

Total drink volume: approximately
 80ml (2⅔oz)
Ideal glass volume: 100–150ml
 (3⅓–5oz)
Glass: chilled coupette or
 Martini glass

This Martini packs a punch. Its clean, crisp and bright flavour suits a London dry gin and my preference here is Beefeater – its balanced citrus notes add a brightness on the nose, while the bitter almond and orris give a little roundness to the overall flavour of the cocktail.

Fill a cocktail tin with cubed ice. Add the gin and dry vermouth and stir approximately 15 times to combine. Double strain into your chilled glass, garnish with an olive or lemon disc or twist that's had its oils expressed over the surface of the liquid and serve.

Note: If you are intrigued by the flavour impact of different gins, try a few Dry Martinis made from different gins, side by side, and take note of what you smell and taste. You'll soon find your favourite gin for making Martinis.

GIN

DRY VERMOUTH

WET GIN MARTINI

50ml (1⅔oz) gin
15ml (½oz) dry vermouth
green olive or disc of lemon peel

Total drink volume: approximately 85ml (2⅔oz plus 1 tsp)
Ideal glass volume: 100–150ml (3⅓–5oz)
Glass: chilled coupette or Martini glass

This is my favourite style of Martini. Though this cocktail does not taste sweet or sour, the dry vermouth does provide a touch of sweetness and acidity, so the increased volume of dry vermouth here creates a less aggressive, more approachable Martini. We are also increasing the volume of dry vermouth aromatics in this cocktail, creating synergy when combined with the gin.

Fill a cocktail tin with cubed ice. Add the gin and dry vermouth and stir approximately 15 times to combine. Double strain into your chilled glass, garnish with an olive or lemon disc that's had its oils expressed over the surface of the liquid and serve.

Note: If you are comparing Wet and Dry Martinis, use the same gin and dry vermouth in both cocktails. That way, the difference in proportions will be the only change in the drink, highlighting what a touch more dry vermouth does to the balance of the cocktail.

GIN

DRY VERMOUTH

DIRTY GIN MARTINI

50ml (1⅔oz) gin

5ml (1 tsp) dry vermouth

10ml (2 tsp) olive brine
   from the jar

2 green olives

Total drink volume: approximately
   85ml (2⅔oz plus 1 tsp)

Ideal glass volume: 100–150ml
   (3⅓–5oz)

Glass: chilled coupette or
   Martini glass

The salinity and savoury notes of an olive become the focus in this cocktail, creating a drink with a touch more texture and an almost leathery note that adds a smoothness to the flavour. Though I wouldn't describe this cocktail as 'heavy' in flavour, if you like more impactful flavours, I recommend you try this.

Fill a cocktail tin with cubed ice. Add the gin, dry vermouth and olive brine and stir approximately 15 times to combine. Double strain into your chilled glass, garnish with 2 olives and serve.

GIN

DRY VERMOUTH

OLIVE BRINE

GIBSON

50ml (1⅔oz) gin
10ml (2 tsp) dry vermouth
1.25ml (¼ tsp) pickled onion
   juice from the jar
2 silver skin pickled cocktail
   onions

Total drink volume:
   approximately 80ml (2⅔oz)
Ideal glass volume:
   100–150ml (3⅓–5oz)
Glass: chilled coupette or
   Martini glass

For this cocktail I've switched my gin preference to Sipsmith – its woody, green aroma works well against the sharpness of the pickled onion. Traditionally this cocktail doesn't contain any pickle juice, but the addition of acid gives it a little complexity and a builds a more savoury flavour profile.

Fill a cocktail tin with cubed ice. Add the gin, dry vermouth and pickled onion juice and stir approximately 15 times to combine. Double strain into your chilled glass, garnish with the onions and serve.

Note: You can purchase small cocktail onions, which are the ideal size. If you struggle to find these, normal small silver skin pickled onions will work. Feel free to omit the pickle juice from the recipe if you feel it's too potent!

GIN

DRY VERMOUTH

PICKLED ONION JUICE FROM THE JAR

GIMLET

50ml (1⅔oz) gin
25ml (⅔oz plus 1 tsp) lime cordial
disc of lime peel

Total drink volume:
   approximately 95ml
   (3oz plus 1 tsp)
Ideal glass volume:
   100–150ml (3⅓–5oz)
Glass: chilled coupette

The Gimlet moves us into a slightly different stirred cocktail space, so if Martinis are still a little intimidating, I recommend you start here, as you'll appreciate the additional sweetness, acid and fruit flavour. I love the simplicity of this recipe – suddenly a bottle of cordial has a whole new function and it's truly delicious.

Fill a cocktail tin with cubed ice. Add the gin and lime cordial and stir approximately 15 times to combine. Double strain into the chilled glass, garnish with a lime disc that's had its oils expressed over the surface of the liquid and serve.

Note: Though this recipe asks for lime cordial, feel free to experiment with any flavour of cordial. Gin has a very adaptable flavour profile – you'll be able to push this drink into different fruit and floral directions through this change. You may also like to make your own cordials.

GIN

LIME CORDIAL

From left to right: Gibson (see page 108), Martinez (see page 115) and Dirty Vodka Martini (see page 113)

VODKA MARTINI

50ml (1⅔oz) vodka
5ml (1 tsp) dry vermouth
green olive or disc of lemon peel

Total drink volume: approximately
   75ml (2⅓oz plus 1 tsp)
Ideal glass volume: 100–150ml
   (3⅓–5oz)
Glass: chilled coupette or
   Martini glass

The beauty of a vodka Martini is its clean and smooth flavour; there is nowhere to hide here, so I recommend you use a good-quality vodka. Rye vodka will produce a slightly deeper, rounder flavour result than wheat, but both work well – it's down to your preference. You'll notice we use less vermouth and therefore have fewer aromatics in a Vodka Martini: this is to keep the focus of this drink on the clean and crisp effect that vodka brings. Finally, don't forget the importance of the garnish; an olive will build on the smoothness of this cocktail, while a lemon disc will add bright aromatics.

Fill a cocktail tin with cubed ice. Add the vodka and dry vermouth and stir approximately 15 times to combine. Double strain into the chilled glass, garnish with an olive or lemon disc that's had its oils expressed over the surface of the liquid and serve.

Note: Feel free to experiment with different types of vodka here and explore how their flavours open up when mixed with dry vermouth.

VODKA

DRY VERMOUTH

DIRTY VODKA MARTINI

50ml (1⅔oz) vodka

5ml (1 tsp) dry vermouth

10ml (2 tsp) olive brine
   from the jar

2 green olives

Total drink volume: approximately
   85ml (2⅔oz plus 1 tsp)

Ideal glass volume: 100–150ml
   (3⅓–5oz)

Glass: chilled coupette or
   Martini glass

When comparing this cocktail to a Dirty Gin Martini (see page 107), you'll notice that the savoury qualities of this drink are more intense and focused. This again is due to the reduction of aromatics as we are not using gin. Therefore, if you are looking for a more savoury-focused cocktail, this style of Martini will be for you.

Fill a cocktail tin with cubed ice. Add the vodka, dry vermouth and olive brine and stir approximately 15 times to combine. Double strain into the chilled glass, garnish with 2 olives and serve.

VODKA

DRY VERMOUTH

OLIVE BRINE

SHERRY MARTINI

50ml (1⅔oz) vodka
15ml (½oz) fino sherry
disc of lemon peel

Total drink volume: approximately
85ml (2⅔oz plus 1 tsp)
Ideal glass volume:
100–150ml (3⅓–5oz)
Glass: chilled coupette or
Martini glass

For a Sherry Martini, my vodka preference switches to wheat; its lighter flavour profile produces a bright-tasting liquid that allows for the sherry to shine through. That said, if you only have rye vodka to hand, it's no problem – the cocktail will still work with this style of vodka.

Fill a cocktail tin with cubed ice. Add the vodka and fino sherry and stir approximately 15 times to combine. Double strain into the chilled glass, garnish with a lemon disc that's had its oils expressed over the surface of the liquid and serve.

Note: I like to use a Manzanilla fino sherry, which is unique to the coastal town of Sanlúcar de Barrameda in southern Spain. These sherries have a nutty taste and slight salinity that works well here. Feel free to experiment with different styles of sherry – most dry sherries will produce good results.

VODKA

FINO SHERRY

MARTINEZ

40ml (1⅓oz) gin
40ml (1⅓oz) sweet vermouth
5ml (1 tsp) maraschino liqueur
4 dashes of Boker's bitters
disc of orange peel

Total drink volume:
   approximately 110ml (3⅔oz)
Ideal glass volume: 100–150ml
   (3⅓–5oz)
Glass: chilled coupette

The Martinez is a classic cocktail that laid the path for the Martinis we know today. Sweet vermouth creates a very different flavour profile for this drink, which perhaps sits closer to the profile of a Manhattan, but retains a crisp and herbaceous note thanks to the combination of botanicals found in the gin and the Boker's bitters. I recommend a balanced citrus gin for this cocktail; a powerfully herbaceous gin would throw it off balance.

Fill a cocktail tin with cubed ice. Add the gin, sweet vermouth, maraschino liqueur and bitters and stir approximately 15 times to combine. Double strain into the chilled glass, garnish with an orange disc that's had its oils expressed over the surface of the liquid and serve.

Note: It is traditional to use Boker's bitters in this cocktail, and if you can get these bitters, do use them. They have a slightly warmer flavour profile that suits this drink. If not, try with Angostura but halve the amount.

 GIN

SWEET VERMOUTH

MARASCHINO LIQUEUR

BOKER'S BITTERS

SWEET MANHATTAN

40ml (1⅓oz) Bourbon
20ml (⅔oz) sweet vermouth
2.5ml (½ tsp) maraschino liqueur
1 dash of Angostura bitters
maraschino cherry

Total drink volume:
   approximately 75ml
   (2⅓oz plus 1 tsp)
Ideal glass volume: 100–150ml
   (3⅓–5oz)
Glass: chilled coupette

A Sweet Manhattan is a great place to start if you are looking to explore Bourbon-based stirred cocktails. Despite its rich, sweet, warm and woody flavour, this cocktail has a dry finish, making you want to go back for more.

Fill a cocktail tin with cubed ice. Add the Bourbon, sweet vermouth, maraschino liqueur and Angostura bitters and stir approximately 15 times to combine. Double strain into the chilled glass, garnish with a maraschino cherry and serve.

Note: Buffalo Trace is a great Bourbon to start with, but do feel free to experiment with your choice, paying attention to how it changes the body and length of flavour in the cocktail.

 BOURBON

SWEET VERMOUTH

 MARASCHINO LIQUEUR

 ANGOSTURA BITTERS

PERFECT MANHATTAN

40ml (1⅓oz) Bourbon
10ml (2 tsp) sweet vermouth
10ml (2 tsp) dry vermouth
1 dash of Angostura bitters
disc of orange peel

Total drink volume: approximately 75ml (2⅓oz plus 1 tsp)
Ideal glass volume: 100–150ml (3⅓–5oz)
Glass: chilled coupette

Lighter and drier than a Sweet Manhattan (see page 117), this cocktail emphasizes the dry, candied citrus notes often found in Bourbon. If your preference is citrus-led flavours, this style of Manhattan will be for you. Note that the overall proportion of vermouth to Bourbon has stayed the same; we have just split the vermouth up into the two styles of sweet and dry. This builds a different flavour profile for this cocktail.

Fill a cocktail tin with cubed ice. Add the Bourbon, sweet vermouth, dry vermouth and Angostura bitters and stir approximately 15 times to combine. Double strain into the chilled glass, garnish with an orange disc that's had its oils expressed over the surface of the liquid and serve.

BOURBON

SWEET VERMOUTH

DRY VERMOUTH

ANGOSTURA BITTERS

RUM SWEET MANHATTAN

40ml (1⅓oz) aged golden rum,
   such as Havana Club Selección
   de Maestros

20ml (⅔oz) sweet vermouth

2.5ml (½ tsp) maraschino liqueur

1 dash of Angostura bitters

maraschino cherry

Total drink volume: approximately
   75ml (2⅓oz plus 1 tsp)

Ideal glass volume: 100–150ml
   (3⅓–5oz)

Glass: chilled coupette

Classic cocktails are versatile, meaning the structure of a Manhattan cocktail will translate to other dark spirits. So if you have a collection of sprits at home that includes aged rum, you can explore this spirit's potential within the structure of a Manhattan.

Fill a cocktail tin with cubed ice. Add the rum, sweet vermouth, maraschino liqueur and Angostura bitters and stir approximately 15 times to combine. Double strain into the chilled glass, garnish with a maraschino cherry and serve.

AGED GOLDEN RUM

SWEET VERMOUTH

MARASCHINO LIQUEUR

ANGOSTURA BITTERS

ROB ROY

40ml (1⅓oz) Scotch whisky

20ml (⅔oz) sweet vermouth

2.5ml (½ tsp) maraschino liqueur

1 dash of Angostura bitters

disc of lemon peel

Total drink volume: approximately 75ml (2⅓oz plus 1 tsp)

Ideal glass volume: 100–150ml (3⅓–5oz)

Glass: chilled coupette

The Rob Roy uses the same recipe as a Sweet Manhattan (see page 117) but switches the Bourbon for Scotch whisky. The result is a cocktail of 'higher pitch' than the Sweet Manhattan. This is a bright, almost honeyed Scotch cocktail, where the flavour profile of the whisky takes centre stage.

Fill a cocktail tin with cubed ice. Add the Scotch whisky, sweet vermouth, maraschino liqueur and Angostura bitters and stir approximately 15 times to combine. Double strain into the chilled glass, garnish with a lemon disc that's had its oils expressed over the surface of the liquid and serve.

Note: The change from an orange to lemon disc is driven by the switch to Scotch whisky, as the aroma of lemon sits better against the Scotch.

 SCOTCH WHISKY

 SWEET VERMOUTH

 MARASCHINO LIQUEUR

 ANGOSTURA BITTERS

HARVARD

40ml (1⅓oz) Cognac
40ml (1⅓oz) sweet vermouth
3 dashes of Angostura bitters
long orange peel

Total drink volume: approximately
   95ml (3oz plus 1 tsp)
Ideal glass volume: 100–150ml
   (3⅓–5oz)
Glass: chilled coupette

The Harvard takes the structure of a Manhattan cocktail and simplifies it. Here, we increase the volume of sweet vermouth and omit the maraschino liqueur, as the fruitiness of the Cognac balances well against the botanicals and aromatics of the vermouth.

Fill a cocktail tin with cubed ice. Add the Cognac, sweet vermouth and Angostura bitters and stir approximately 15 times to combine. Double strain into the chilled glass, garnish with a long orange peel that's had its oils expressed over the surface of the liquid and serve.

Note: Historical recipes for this cocktail ask for the addition of a dash of soda water to the finished drink. I've removed this, which is not uncommon in modern-day bars. The soda water doesn't make the drink fizzy, yet it's no longer 'flat' either, which makes for a strange experience. Do keep an eye on the dilution of this cocktail; you need it to open up the flavours of the ingredients, which would have been the function of the soda water.

COGNAC

SWEET VERMOUTH

ANGOSTURA BITTERS

EL PRESIDENTE

40ml (1⅓oz) aged golden rum,
   such as **Havana Club Selección**
   de Maestros
20ml (⅔oz) sweet vermouth
10ml (2 tsp) triple sec
5ml (1 tsp) Grenadine
   (see page 59)
twist of orange peel

Total drink volume:
   approximately 95ml
   (3oz plus 1 tsp)
Ideal glass volume: 100–150ml
   (3⅓–5oz)
Glass: chilled coupette

Here, through the change to aged rum, we flip the structure created in the Sweet Manhattan (see page 117) and build on it through the additional flavours of triple sec and grenadine. The grenadine's red fruit aroma underpins the wine base of the sweet vermouth, while the triple sec adds a bright citrus note. Overall, there is a great depth of flavour in this rum cocktail.

Fill a cocktail tin with cubed ice. Add the rum, sweet vermouth, triple sec and grenadine and stir approximately 15 times to combine. Double strain into the chilled glass, garnish with an orange twist that's had its oils expressed over the surface of the liquid and serve.

☐ AGED GOLDEN RUM,

■ SWEET VERMOUTH

☐ TRIPLE SEC

■ GRENADINE

OLD FASHIONED

**5ml (1 tsp) Sugar Syrup
(see page 59)**
4 dashes of Angostura bitters
50ml (1⅔oz) Bourbon
long orange peel
**4 ice cubes or 1 large cube,
to serve**

Total drink volume: approximately
70ml (2⅓oz)
Ideal glass volume: 250ml (8½oz)
Glass: chilled rocks glass

This is an iconic cocktail that is simple in its flavour delivery, resulting in an elegant sipping drink. As we focus on the qualities of the Bourbon, pick your favourite and explore its flavour profile through the addition of bitters, sugar, orange and a little dilution.

Fill a cocktail tin with cubed ice. Add the sugar syrup, Angostura bitters and 25ml (⅔oz plus 1 tsp) of the Bourbon and stir 10 times. Add the remaining 25ml (⅔oz plus 1 tsp) of Bourbon and stir a further 10 times. Double strain into the chilled glass, add the ice, garnish with a long orange peel that's had its oils expressed over the surface of the liquid and serve.

Note: In this cocktail, the sugar and bitters are added first, along with just half the Bourbon. This is to ensure that the sugar and bitters dissolve and integrate with the Bourbon. The remaining Bourbon is then added to the drink so that we layer up the flavour profile of the Bourbon and ensure the drink is not over-diluted.

 BOURBON

 SUGAR SYRUP

 ANGOSTURA BITTERS

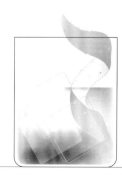

SCOTCH OLD FASHIONED

3.75ml (¾ tsp) Sugar Syrup
   (see page 59)
3 dashes of Angostura bitters
50ml (1⅔oz) Scotch whisky
long lemon peel
4 ice cubes or 1 large cube,
   to serve

Total drink volume:
   approximately 70ml (2⅓oz)
Ideal glass volume: 250ml (8½oz)
Glass: chilled rocks glass

If you are a Scotch lover, this Old Fashioned will be your go-to. There is less sugar and bitters in this version to balance the dryness of the Scotch, ensuring these two ingredients don't dominate and overpower the cocktail.

Fill a cocktail tin with cubed ice. Add the sugar syrup, Angostura bitters and 25ml (⅔oz plus 1 tsp) of the Scotch whisky and stir 10 times. Add the remaining 25ml (⅔oz plus 1 tsp) of Scotch whisky and stir a further 10 times. Double strain into the chilled glass, add the ice, garnish with a long lemon peel that's had its oils expressed over the surface of the liquid and serve.

Note: You may like to try the traditional 5ml (1 tsp) of sugar syrup and 4 dashes of Angostura in this cocktail. See what you think and examine how these ingredients work together so that you can find a balance to suit you and your selected Scotch.

■ SCOTCH WHISKY

□ SUGAR SYRUP

■ ANGOSTURA BITTERS

RUM OLD FASHIONED

5ml (1 tsp) Sugar Syrup
(see page 59)
4 dashes of orange bitters
50ml (1⅔oz) aged golden rum,
such as Havana Club Selección
de Maestros
long twist of orange peel
4 ice cubes or 1 large cube,
to serve

Total drink volume: approximately
70ml (2⅓oz)
Ideal glass volume: 250ml (8½oz)
Glass: chilled rocks glass

The structure of an Old Fashioned cocktail is so versatile, we can easily jump into different spirit categories with it. Here, a twist in the flavour of the bitters amplifies the smooth, aromatic flavour of the rum. When compared with the Bourbon version (see page 124), this is a sweeter and richer Old Fashioned.

Fill a cocktail tin with cubed ice. Add the sugar syrup, orange bitters and 25ml (⅔oz plus 1 tsp) of the rum and stir 10 times. Add the remaining 25ml (⅔oz plus 1 tsp) of rum and stir a further 10 times. Double strain into the chilled glass, add the ice, garnish with a long orange twist that's had its oils expressed over the surface of the liquid and serve.

Note: You may like to try this drink using half Angostura bitters and half orange bitters. I like the lightness of just the orange bitters, as it allows the rum to shine through.

AGED GOLDEN RUM

SUGAR SYRUP

ORANGE BITTERS

VODKA OLD FASHIONED

2.5ml (½ tsp) Sugar Syrup
   (see page 59)
3 dashes of grapefruit bitters
50ml (1⅔oz) vodka
long twist of pink grapefruit peel
4 ice cubes or 1 large cube,
   to serve

Total drink volume: approximately
   85ml (2⅔oz plus 1 tsp)
Ideal glass volume: 250ml (8½oz)
Glass: chilled rocks glass

Vodka's clean and smooth flavour profile can be taken advantage of in an Old Fashioned-style cocktail. The results are very different to a traditional Bourbon Old Fashioned (see page 124), but if vodka is your go-to spirit, this cocktail's structure will have something to offer you. It's a slightly sweeter cocktail and the flavour profile of the bitters and aromatics in the garnish take centre stage.

Fill a cocktail tin with cubed ice. Add the sugar syrup, grapefruit bitters and 25ml (⅔oz plus 1 tsp) of the vodka and stir 15 times to combine. Add the remaining 25ml (⅔oz plus 1 tsp) of vodka and stir a further 10 times. Double strain into the chilled glass, add the ice, garnish with a long pink grapefruit twist that's had its oils expressed over the surface of the liquid and serve.

Note: Traditionally, Angostura bitters are used in an Old Fashioned, but as vodka has such a clean structure, we need to consider which bitters will best complement it, hence the switch to a lighter grapefruit bitters. Keep this in mind and feel free to explore the potential of different lighter, aromatic cocktail bitters, or even absinthe.

VODKA

SUGAR SYRUP

GRAPEFRUIT BITTERS

TEQUILA OLD FASHIONED

10ml (2 tsp) Agave Syrup
(see page 59)

4 dashes of orange bitters

50ml (1⅔oz) tequila reposado

long orange peel

4 ice cubes or 1 large cube,
to serve

Total drink volume: approximately
80ml (2⅔oz)

Ideal glass volume: 250ml (8½oz)

Glass: chilled rocks glass

With the switch to tequila, we balance the flavour of the cocktail with the aroma of the bitters and the addition of a sweetening agent. Agave syrup provides a sweetness to balance the cocktail as well as an overall flavour to reinforce that of the agave in the tequila. Orange bitters provide a lighter structure, which is important – Angostura's intensity would overpower and throw the balance of this cocktail off.

Fill a cocktail tin with cubed ice. Add the agave syrup, orange bitters and 25ml (⅔oz plus 1 tsp) of the tequila reposado and stir 10 times. Add the remaining 25ml (⅔oz plus 1 tsp) of tequila reposado and stir a further 10 times. Double strain into the chilled glass, add the ice, garnish with a long orange peel that's had its oils expressed over the surface of the liquid and serve.

Note: I've used a tequila reposado for this cocktail, as it is aged in oak barrels. It provides a little more structured flavour to the liquid, which suits this drink. This is something you can experiment with. Try a tequila añejo if you would like a stronger oak flavour, as this will have been aged in oak barrels for a minimum of one year.

 TEQUILA REPOSADO

 AGAVE SYRUP

 ORANGE BITTERS

MEZCAL OLD FASHIONED

10ml (2 tsp) Agave Syrup
(see page 59)

4 dashes of grapefruit bitters

25ml (⅔oz plus 1 tsp) mezcal
espadin

25ml (⅔oz plus 1 tsp) tequila
reposado

long grapefruit peel

4 ice cubes or 1 large cube,
to serve

Total drink volume: approximately
70ml (2⅓oz)

Ideal glass volume: 250ml (8½oz)

Glass: chilled rocks glass

Here, our core structure is the same as the Tequila Old Fashioned (see page 129), but we evolve the flavour profile of this drink with the addition of mezcal and its smoky, resinous notes. The world of mezcal is vast, with each producer providing a unique flavour profile for you to explore. For this recipe, I have used an espadin, as its slightly sweet and modest flavour creates a subtle Mezcal Old Fashioned.

Fill a cocktail tin with cubed ice. Add the agave syrup, grapefruit bitters, mezcal espadin and tequila reposado and stir approximately 20 times. Double strain into the chilled glass, add the ice, garnish with a long grapefruit peel that's had its oils expressed over the surface of the liquid and serve.

Note: The method of making an Old Fashioned has changed slightly here, as we add both spirits at the same time. This is so that we may fully integrate their flavours during the mixing process. Orange bitters also work well in this cocktail.

 MEZCAL ESPADIN

 TEQUILA REPOSADO

 AGAVE SYRUP

 GRAPEFRUIT BITTERS

SAZERAC RYE

5ml (1 tsp) Pernod absinthe

50ml (1⅔oz) rye whiskey

6.25ml (1¼ tsp) Sugar Syrup
   (see page 59)

5 dashes of Peychaud's bitters

discarded lemon disc

Total drink volume: approximately
   65ml (2oz plus 1 tsp)

Ideal glass volume: 250ml (8½oz)

Glass: chilled rocks glass

Traditionally, the Sazerac is stirred, but while this might be something the cocktail world will find controversial, I like a shaken Sazerac. A short, sharp shake integrates the flavours of the highly aromatic bitters with the rye and sugar, as well as adding a little texture to the drink. I feel this helps to open up and deliver the flavour of this cocktail. I've included both methods of making so that you can explore how a technique changes a cocktail.

Stirred method: Firstly, add the absinthe to the chilled glass. Fill a cocktail tin with cubed ice. Add the rye whiskey, sugar syrup and Peychaud's bitters to the tin and stir approximately 10 times to combine. Pick up the rocks glass and swill the absinthe around in it, aiming to coat the walls of the glass as much as possible, then discard any remaining absinthe. Double strain the Sazerac into the absinthe-washed glass and express the oils from the lemon disc over the surface of the liquid, discard it and serve.

Shaken method: Follow the instructions above to wash the chilled glass with absinthe. Fill the larger half of a cocktail shaker with cubed ice. Add the rye whiskey, sugar syrup and Peychaud's bitters, seal the shaker and short, hard shake. Double strain the Sazerac into the absinthe-washed glass and express the oils from the lemon disc over the surface of the liquid, discard it and serve.

Note: Pay attention to the sugar here – 6.25ml (1¼ tsp) is a bit of a funny measurement, but I personally feel it suits the drink. You may like to go up or down in sugar, but not below 5ml (1 tsp) or above 10ml (2 tsp).

 RYE WHISKEY

SUGAR SYRUP

PEYCHAUD'S BITTERS

PERNOD ABSINTHE

SAZERAC COGNAC

5ml (1 tsp) Pernod absinthe
50ml (1⅔oz) Cognac
6.25ml (1¼ tsp) Sugar Syrup
   (see page 59)
5 dashes of Peychaud's bitters
discarded lemon disc

Total drink volume: approximately
   65ml (2oz plus 1 tsp)
Ideal glass volume: 250ml (8½oz)
Glass: chilled rocks glass

The Sazerac is one of the classic cocktails where a spirit choice is normally offered – rye or Cognac. Cognac gives a slightly sweeter, smoother and very delicious Sazerac.

Stirred method: Firstly, add the absinthe to the chilled glass. Fill a cocktail tin with cubed ice. Add the Cognac, sugar syrup and Peychaud's bitters to the tin and stir approximately 10 times to combine. Pick up the rocks glass and swill the absinthe around in it, aiming to coat the walls of the glass as much as possible, then discard any remaining absinthe. Double strain the Sazerac into the absinthe-washed glass and express the oils from the lemon disc over the surface of the liquid, discard it and serve.

Shaken method: Follow the instructions above to wash the chilled glass with absinthe. Fill the larger half of a cocktail shaker with cubed ice. Add the Cognac, sugar syrup and Peychaud's bitters, seal the shaker and short, hard shake. Double strain the Sazerac into the absinthe-washed glass and express the oils from the lemon disc over the surface of the liquid, discard it and serve.

COGNAC

SUGAR SYRUP

PEYCHAUD'S BITTERS

PERNOD ABSINTHE

CHAPTER 8:
BITTER COCKTAILS

Bitter is complex and often divides people, making it one of the most intriguing of the basic tastes. Our genes determine our sensitivity to bitter through the number of bitter taste receptors we have in our mouths. A greater number of receptors means we will be more sensitive to bitter, perceiving it as an overwhelming and possibly unpleasant experience. Yet with time we can work to overrule this predisposition and adapt our palates to accept and enjoy bitter tastes. Our daily coffee routine is a great example of this in action. We have all become more accustomed to bitter through the small food and drink choices we make.

Despite bitter being one of the most controversial of the basic tastes, the popularity of bitter cocktails has grown dramatically in recent years; the welcoming Spritz (see page 149) as well as the more punchy Negroni (see page 140) went from niche to mainstream in a short space of time, introducing the ritual of aperitivo culture to a wider audience.

Before we delve deeper into the structure of bitter cocktails, I'd like to highlight how diverse this cocktail category is; there really is something for everyone to enjoy and create an aperitivo moment with. This section includes built, stirred and long drinks, giving us varying alcohol contents, aromatic concentrations and textures to explore. The cocktails are very logical in construction, simple in their method of preparation and often pair well with salty, savoury snacks – making these cocktails go-to welcome drinks if you are hosting.

NOT ALL BITTER IS MADE EQUAL

This cocktail category's foundation is set by the flavour qualities contained in bitter spirits such as Italian red bitter liqueurs. To make each of these products, a wide range of herbs, flowers, bitter woods and citrus peels are infused into alcohol and water. Sugar is then added to the resulting liquid, creating a bitter-sweet liqueur for us to work with. You'll notice that none of the recipes in this chapter require any additional sugar, as we conveniently have the sweetness we need already included in the spirit.

For most of these liqueurs, the exact botanical recipes are kept secret – some brands don't disclose any details. But what we do know is that these products are highly aromatized and intense in flavour, which is exciting for us. Bitter cocktails are about so much more than their bitter taste; they are about layering flavour. It's important to realize that different botanicals impart different bitter tastes; not all bitter is made equal. So, as always, first taste your bitter liqueurs on their own. If you have more than one bitter liqueur or a vermouth (which also has a slight bitter note) to hand, then taste these products side by side to help you to highlight the flavour qualities of each. Pay attention to what you perceive and the intensity of bitterness that you taste. The description of common bitter botanicals overleaf may help you to identify the varying bitter taste qualities within your liquids.

BITTER TASTE DESCRIPTORS

Bitter orange: green bitterness as if from unripe fruit

Gentian: dry and woody, deep and powerful bitterness

Orris: delicate powdery bitterness

Thyme: not so much bitter but more 'cutting' or astringent in taste

What is intriguing and useful about these bitter botanicals is that they aren't just bitter and we can build flavour connections with other ingredients through the complexity of their aromatic profile. Using tradition, instinct and logic – as well as tools such as food-pairing books and websites – we can look to find other ingredients to complement the aromatic profile of these bitter ingredients, then feed these into our cocktails. Fresh citrus fruits and rhubarb will complement and add brightness to bitter orange, florals such as rose and orange blossom will sit well against orris and we can build complexity through the addition of other green herbs. These are common ingredients you'll often find used in bitter cocktails. Though this chapter isn't focused on bespoke cocktail recipes, it's this thought process and knowledge that a bartender uses to create new drinks, and it's worth keeping this in mind next time you visit a bar and order a bespoke cocktail. Take a look at the aromatic profiles below for more details on each of the bitter botanicals.

AROMATIC DESCRIPTORS

Bitter orange: warm, tangy citrus

Gentian: astringent, very subtle aroma

Orris: delicate, powdery floral aroma reminiscent of raspberries

Thyme: herbaceous, warm green terpene aroma with a subtle lemon note

Finally, what we have discussed here doesn't just apply to Italian red bitter liqueurs. Dry and sweet vermouth and the wider range of amaros have a similar botanical structure, hence their frequent use in bitter cocktails. Gin's aromatic profile also has parallels with this category of spirit, which is why it works so well in a Negroni.

CONSIDERING A BITTER COCKTAIL'S TASTE

In the Champagne cocktails chapter, we learned that simplicity is key and that bubbles give texture to a drink. In the stirred cocktail chapter, we discussed the importance of dilution, temperature and the impact of a garnish on the perception of a liquid. These points can and should all be applied to the bitter cocktail category – in fact, to all cocktails. They are key structural elements that you need to keep in mind at all times. Here, simplicity is important, as the products we use in bitter cocktails are flavour dense; a little dilution goes a long way in opening up the flavour profiles of these drinks. And in a sense, that is all we really need to create a new experience; the products we are using here are totally unique in their offering and on their own produce some of the most aromatic and flavoursome cocktails. A citrus garnish is normally enough to brighten and highlight the citrus notes held within the glass.

Temperature plays an important role when we look at the perception of sweetness in bitter drinks. Cool temperatures suppress our taste buds, so we perceive sugar as being less sweet. This is of benefit to us here, as the ingredients we are working with are sweet. Serving these drinks over ice offers us the opportunity to make the sweetness of bitter cocktails more palatable.

A new structural element for us to explore here, though, is the relationship between bitter, salt and umami. In a sense, aperitivo cocktails have an additional garnish and that is the snack that is offered alongside these drinks during the aperitivo hour – olives, cheese and cured meats are a few of the more common options. It's the salty and savoury qualities of these foods that offer us a new point of view on balancing a cocktail. Salt suppresses our perception of bitterness. It also helps to cut through sweetness and amplify the overall flavours we are experiencing. So a salty snack with a bitter drink helps to make the bitterness more approachable in taste and highlights the botanical-rich flavours of the liquid. Umami works in a similar way through the addition of savouriness, adding another dimension of taste to our experience that gives our taste buds, and therefore our brains, more to engage with. Keep this in mind next time you enjoy or offer a snack with a cocktail.

THE RITUAL OF THE APERITIVO HOUR

Traditionally, an aperitivo is a bitter cocktail consumed before dinner. Bitter comes into play in these drinks, as it's believed to help stimulate the appetite. In Italy, a whole ritual has grown out of this tradition, with the aperitivo hour referring to the early hours of the evening when a delicious and approachable cocktail is consumed alongside light bar snacks such as olives, nuts, cured meats and cheese. For a lot of people, aperitivo cocktails tap into nostalgic moments from holidays or warm summer evenings. It's this emotional 'pull' and elegance of the Italian culture of food and drink that makes this category of drinks perfect for hosting and welcoming guests. Our pivot point is the transportive effect of the ritual and the opportunity to relive a holiday moment or embrace the traditions of Italian culture, bringing a touch of magic to our aperitivo hour.

INGREDIENTS FOR BITTER COCKTAILS

FROM YOUR DRINKS CABINET

Italian red bitter liqueur, such as Campari

Aperol

Bourbon

Gin

Mezcal

Prosecco

Sweet vermouth

ADDITIONAL ITEMS

Fresh oranges

Soda water

MILANO TORINO

25ml (⅔oz plus 1 tsp) Campari

25ml (⅔oz plus 1 tsp) sweet vermouth

orange slice

cubed ice, to serve

Total drink volume: 50ml (1⅔oz)

Ideal glass volume: 250ml (8½oz)

Glass: rocks glass

The Milano Torino is the cornerstone of aperitivo hour. Its equal-parts recipe forms the founding structure for cocktails such as the Negroni and its numerous spirit twists (see pages 140–143), the Americano (see page 144) and Spagliato (see page 146). These cocktails have two things in common: they all build on the combined flavour profile of Italian red bitter liqueurs and sweet vermouth, and these two ingredients are measured in equal parts in each drink. This is great news for us, as it makes it easy to remember recipes and gives us the opportunity to explore how the flavour of these two products changes with one simple ingredient addition or switch. Keep this in mind when you explore the following cocktail recipes.

Fill the glass with cubed ice, add the Campari and sweet vermouth and stir 5 times to mix. Garnish with a slice of orange and serve.

 CAMPARI

 SWEET VERMOUTH

NEGRONI

25ml (⅔oz plus 1 tsp) Campari
25ml (⅔oz plus 1 tsp) sweet
vermouth
25ml (⅔oz plus 1 tsp) gin
orange slice or peel
cubed ice, to serve

Total drink volume: approximately
100ml (3⅓oz)
Ideal glass volume: 250ml (8½oz)
Glass: rocks glass

*The botanicals used to make gin complement those used in Italian bitter
liqueurs and sweet vermouth, making this cocktail incredibly aromatic as well
as a little stronger in ABV.*

Fill a cocktail tin with cubed ice. Add the Campari, sweet vermouth and
gin to the tin and stir 15 times to mix and dilute. Fill the glass with cubed
ice. Double strain the drink into the glass, garnish with an orange slice or
orange peel and serve.

Note: A balanced citrus gin such as Beefeater London Dry will perfectly
complement the flavour profile of Campari and sweet vermouth. But do feel
free to experiment; try a few different gins, keeping flavour pairings in mind,
and find your preference.

 CAMPARI

 SWEET VERMOUTH

 GIN

MEZCAL NEGRONI

25ml (⅔oz plus 1 tsp) **Campari**

25ml (⅔oz plus 1 tsp) **sweet vermouth**

20ml (⅔oz) **mezcal**

orange slice

cubed ice, to serve

Total drink volume: approximately 95ml (3oz plus 1 tsp)

Ideal glass volume: 250ml (8½oz)

Glass: rocks glass

As the founding ingredients in the Milano Torino (see page 139) produce a robust flavour experience, we have enough structure to explore some quite powerful additions such as smokiness, which is where mezcal comes into play with this twist on the classic gin Negroni (see page 140).

Fill a cocktail tin with cubed ice. Add the Campari, sweet vermouth and mezcal to the tin and stir 15 times to mix and dilute. Fill the glass with cubed ice. Double strain the drink into the glass, garnish with an orange slice and serve.

Note: Mezcal has a delicious smoky aroma profile, but it is powerful, so to keep the overall balance true to a Negroni, we need to reduce how much mezcal we add by 5ml (1 tsp). This is also where personal preference comes in; you can change the volume of mezcal to make a more or less intense cocktail, but change only that. Retain the founding Milano Torino structure to keep the balance of sweet, bitter and aromatics correct.

 CAMPARI

 SWEET VERMOUTH

 MEZCAL

BOULEVARDIER

40ml (1⅓oz) Bourbon
20ml (⅔oz) Campari
20ml (⅔oz) sweet vermouth
twist of orange peel

Total drink volume: approximately
  100ml (3⅓oz)
Ideal glass volume: 150–250ml
  (5–8½oz)
Glass: chilled coupette

Here, the swap from gin to Bourbon creates a perfectly balanced bitter cocktail. Its flavour is less intimidating than you may think, as the sweet rye notes of the Bourbon add a smoothness to this drink.

Fill a cocktail tin with cubed ice. Add the Bourbon, Campari and sweet vermouth and stir 20 times to mix and dilute. Double strain into the chilled glass, garnish with an orange twist and serve.

Note: Most Bourbons will suit this cocktail – you can add depth via a warm and rich option or keep the cocktail a little lighter and fruiter by going with a brighter Bourbon such as Maker's Mark. Note here that we have double the volume of Bourbon to Campari and sweet vermouth. As Bourbon has such a smooth flavour profile, we need a little more of it to stand up to our two founding bitter cocktail ingredients.

CAMPARI

SWEET VERMOUTH

BOURBON

AMERICANO

25ml (⅔oz plus 1 tsp) Campari

25ml (⅔oz plus 1 tsp) sweet vermouth

splash of soda water

orange slice or wheel

cubed ice, to serve

Total drink volume: 75ml (2⅓oz plus 1 tsp)

Ideal glass volume: 250ml (8½oz)

Glass: rocks glass or small highball

Through the addition of soda water, we open up the flavour profile of the Campari and sweet vermouth, as well as soften the impact of the bitter-sweet taste of this cocktail's founding ingredients.

Fill the glass with cubed ice. Add the Campari and sweet vermouth and stir gently to mix. Add a splash of soda water and stir once more. Garnish with an orange slice and serve.

Note: You may wish to serve this cocktail with a small bottle of soda water on the side so that your guests can add as much or as little soda as they personally prefer.

CAMPARI

SWEET VERMOUTH

SODA WATER

SPAGLIATO

25ml (⅔oz plus 1 tsp) Campari

25ml (⅔oz plus 1 tsp) sweet vermouth

splash of Prosecco

orange slice

cubed ice, to serve

Total drink volume: 75ml (2⅓oz plus 1 tsp)

Ideal glass volume: 250ml (8½oz)

Glass: rocks glass or small highball

Building on the structure of the Americano (see page 144), here the switch from soda water to Prosecco adds a touch of acidity and a slight green fruit note that brightens the flavour of this cocktail.

Fill the glass with cubed ice. Add the Campari and sweet vermouth and stir gently to mix. Add a splash of Prosecco and stir once more. Garnish with an orange slice and serve.

Note: This cocktail is, in a sense, a cousin of the Spritz (see page 149). So if you are a fan of a Spritz cocktail, do try this and consider the added complexity the sweet vermouth brings.

CAMPARI

SWEET VERMOUTH

PROSECCO

BATCHED MILANO TORINO

250ml (8½oz) Campari
250ml (8½oz) sweet vermouth

Batch volume: 500ml (17oz)
Individual serves: 10
Total drink volume: depends on finished cocktail
Ideal glass volume: 250ml (8½oz)
Glass: depends on finished cocktail
Batch shelf life: 1 week

This batched recipe has a slightly different function to the others in this book (see pages 220–223). As the Milano Torino forms our founding structure for bitter cocktails, we can pre-mix the Campari and sweet vermouth so that we save on a step when it comes to making large numbers of Milano Torinos, Negronis, Mezcal Negronis, Boulevardiers, Americanos or Spagliatos (see pages 139–146). Note there is no water added in this recipe – we will continue to stir or build our bitter cocktails over ice.

Add the Campari and sweet vermouth to a suitably sized jug and stir to combine. Keep in the jug or decant into a bottle and store in the fridge to chill down. When serving, follow your selected recipe, using 50ml (1⅔oz) from this pre-mixed bottle in place of 25ml (⅔oz plus 1 tsp) each of Campari and sweet vermouth.

 CAMPARI

 SWEET VERMOUTH

SPRITZ

50ml (1⅔oz) Aperol
75ml (2½oz plus 1 tsp) Prosecco
25ml (⅔oz plus 1 tsp) soda water
orange slice
cubed ice, to serve

Total drink volume: 150ml (5oz)
Ideal glass volume: 300ml (10oz)
Glass: wine glass

There are many different types of bitter liqueur. Here, we change our spirit base and, therefore, the structure of the cocktail, yet due to the qualities of the Aperol, we retain a bitter-sweet flavour profile. Aperol on its own has a fruitier rhubarb flavour and is a little sweeter. If you are new to drinking bitter cocktails and the recipes so far have sounded a little intimidating, this may be a good place to start introducing your palate to bitter.

Fill the glass with cubed ice. Add the Aperol, top with the Prosecco and soda water and stir gently to mix. Garnish with an orange slice and serve.

Note: You can substitute the soda water with more Prosecco. The drink will be a little rounder and sharper in flavour.

APEROL

PROSECCO

SODA WATER

CHAPTER 9:
SOUR COCKTAILS

There is something to be said about making cocktails for one simple reason – fun. While exploring the structure of cocktails, it's easy to turn these drinks into a serious endeavour and overlook the fact that cocktails, whether you consume them at home or in a bar, should be fun. Cocktails have the power to transport, feed into your mood and change the tone of your night. If Champagne cocktails are about celebration, stirred cocktails evoke a classical elegance and bitter drinks speak to our summer holiday aperitivo hour, sour cocktails are all about being playful. I have to confess, I love sour cocktails and I know I'm not alone. In this chapter, while we'll explore what happens to the structure of a cocktail when the focus is switched to the basic taste of sour, we'll also try to unwrap what it is that makes a sour cocktail so much fun.

SOUR BECOMES OUR CORE

At the start of my cocktail-making career, I had a lot to learn about spirits, their uses and flavour profiles. Many of them I'd never tried before. However, I already had an understanding of what sour, as a basic taste, was. So when it came to making my first sour cocktail, I had a familiar focus point and this led to a key realization: the importance of balance. Yes, a sour cocktail should taste sour; this is the signature for the drinks found in this category. But sour is a powerful taste and will dominate a liquid, which is not necessarily a pleasant experience. I had a small epiphany, as a novice, that the sugar in a sour cocktail was just as important as the lemon or lime juice. The first Whiskey Sour I had made an impact on me; I could clearly see the structure of a cocktail in action. Each ingredient I added to the cocktail shaker had a function that logically built upon its predecessor. I visualized each ingredient 'stepping' up to the next, creating a cocktail that to me felt totally complete.

The logic of a classic Whiskey Sour (see page 171) makes its recipe quite easy to remember. We have the first base step of whiskey: 50ml. Then a step half the size of that: 25ml of fresh lemon juice, which is a logical volume if we want the sour taste of the lemon juice to stand up against the flavour of the whiskey. Then 25ml of egg white – easy to remember, as I've still got a 25ml jigger in my hand. Now I have the same volume of other ingredients in the cocktail shaker as I do whiskey. Yes, the egg white has a slightly different function in this drink – we need it for texture and not taste – but I've got 100ml of liquid in my cocktail shaker and only half of it is whiskey. A single 15ml measuring spoon of sugar syrup takes us up a level to our next step. The sugar is a little over half the volume of the lemon juice, meaning sour is still leading as a basic taste, but its blow has been softened. I also feel that the sugar is doing something else in this cocktail. I see it as the 'glue' that binds all of the other ingredients together to help make the liquid one whole; without sugar we'd have a messy fight between the flavour of whisky and the taste of sour. Finally, two dashes of Angostura bitters create our pinnacle top step and provide a little extra 'seasoning' to our drink.

Of course, this is my personal thought process and perhaps says more about the way I think than anything else. But I hope that as you work through the cocktails in this chapter you'll start to get an idea of the balance and flavour of the drinks without even having to make them. I find the flavour profiles of sour cocktails very easy to imagine and it comes down to the fact that sour, as a basic taste, is our core.

2 DASHES OF ANGOSTURA BITTERS
15ML SUGAR SYRUP

25ML EGG WHITE

25ML LEMON JUICE

50ML WHISKY

THE VALUE OF FOAM

All sours have texture. The physical act of shaking these drinks changes the structure of the liquid, aerating it and providing a slightly different, almost lighter, softer texture on the palate. However, add egg white to a sour and the result is magical. These cocktails tend to snowball in a bar, meaning that as soon as a tray of sours goes out to a table, those guests become centre stage. Everyone else wants to know what they are drinking and would like the same. I blame that enticing-looking foam on top of the liquid. In my eyes, nothing beats the textural sensation of a soft, fluffy foam that breaks to reveal the flavourful delights of the liquid held underneath. Maybe the foam creates an element of transformation that intrigues.

Liquid goes into a cocktail shaker, is shaken once on its own, then ice is added and it's all shaken again. What comes out is, in a loose sense, a fairly solid structure on a liquid. That's kind of magical. I wonder if the time and energy it takes achieving this double shake makes a sour more desirable and therefore valued? That double shake takes its toll – it's exhausting! I rarely make sours for myself, but when I'm out, I do order them and value these cocktails even more. I know someone has gone to all of that effort for me.

Egg white is key to making foam, as it provides us with a protein structure that will trap air and create a network of stable bubbles. As Harold McGee describes in his fantastic book *On Food and Cooking*, 'Stress builds protein solidarity...the key to the stable egg foam is the tendency of the proteins to unfold and bond to each other when they're subjected to physical stress. In a foam this creates a kind of reinforcement for the bubble walls, the culinary equivalent of quick-setting cement.' The stress here is the method of shaking, which aerates the egg whites and enables them to work their magic and create a foam. Note the impact of ice on a foam: the cool temperature does change and reduce the foaming capability of egg white. This is why we have a method with two shakes – the first shake without ice is when the egg white does most of its work.

If you can't consume eggs, you don't need to miss out. Vegan foaming substitutes are easily available and produce good results. I find it useful to have a bottle of one of these products to hand at home, just in case I'm out of eggs and crave a foamy sour.

BUILDING THE FUN FACTOR

There is no doubt that cocktails become fun when we drink them with company or in a specific location designed to entertain us. But I think there is another reason why sours are fun, and I'd like to explore this through a flavour association. While thinking about sour as our core, it struck me that the combination of sour and sweet, as basic tastes, happens in two of the most playful foods we eat: fruit and sweets. By no means am I saying that we don't experience the combination of sour and sweet in other foods; we do. But I believe there is something specific that happens when we decide to eat fruit and sweets, and I'm curious to explore if this association transfers to a sour cocktail.

If you grew up, like I did, only eating generic apples, oranges and pears, then any fruit that is not one of these three is exciting! I vividly remember the first time I saw a lychee in a supermarket, begging to be allowed to try one. It wasn't that my family didn't like fruit, it was just that exotic fruit was expensive. Perhaps this again says more about me. But I think it is these experiences in our lives that help us to build a value and pleasure system for the foods we eat. Going to a supermarket while on family holidays in France was like going to a theme park, something I still feel when I'm abroad. If we take this point of view, which I hope you can relate to, then eating a piece of fruit takes on a different meaning – it's adventurous and therefore fun. Sours intrinsically have a fruity flavour from the lemon or lime juice, but it's not uncommon for sour cocktails to build on this base fruit flavour with another fruity ingredient, such as a liqueur.

There is really nothing quite like the experience of sweets. Having a packet of sweets in your hand is like holding a bundle of little jewels that hit with an intense sweet, sour and often fruity flavour. It's something we crave as children and possibly as adults too. Nostalgia plays its part here. A favourite sweet can, in seconds, take us back to a past experience. So this is my second thought as to why sours are fun – although they aren't sweets, they do play with the same flavour profiles and have the power to evoke nostalgia. Pear Drop Sour, anyone?

A PRACTICAL NOTE

As you should now know, in a bar setting, time and physical impact when delivering cocktails is always a consideration. There is no getting around the fact that sour cocktails take time and energy to make. Be conscious of this if hosting and only offer one shaken drink on your menu. Ensure you have another drink to hand that you can quickly and easily serve, buying you time while you are busy shaking those sours. Fingers crossed, you'll have a guest who's mesmerized by the transformation, will want to learn how to make a delicious sour cocktail and will offer to help you!

INGREDIENTS FOR SOUR COCKTAILS

SOUR COCKTAILS

FROM YOUR DRINKS CABINET

Apricot liqueur

Cognac

Gin

Light rum

Maraschino liqueur

Mezcal

Scotch whisky

Tequila blanco

Triple sec

Vodka

ADDITIONAL ITEMS

Agave Syrup (see page 59)

Caster sugar

Cranberry juice

Fresh lemons

Fresh limes

Fresh pink grapefruits

Maraschino cherries

Sugar Syrup (see page 59)

SOURS WITH ADDED TEXTURE

FROM YOUR DRINKS CABINET

Amaretto

Angostura bitters

Bourbon

Dry vermouth

Gin

Red wine

Scotch whisky

Triple sec

ADDITIONAL ITEMS

Caster sugar

Egg whites

Fresh lemons

Orgeat (see page 60)

Raspberry Syrup (see page 60)

Sugar Syrup (see page 59)

GIN DAISY

50ml (1⅔oz) gin

25ml (⅔oz plus 1 tsp) lemon juice

15ml (½oz) triple sec

10ml (2 tsp) Sugar Syrup
  (see page 59)

twist of lemon peel

Total drink volume: 120ml (4oz)

Ideal glass volume: 150–250ml
  (5–8½oz)

Glass: chilled large coupette

When it comes to sour cocktails, the Gin Daisy is bright and alive with a citrus-led sour taste. Here, the triple sec reinforces the flavour of lemon juice, building a vibrant fresh note that sits very naturally against sour, as a taste, as well as the structure of gin (especially if you're working with a citrus-led gin). That said, the pairing of ingredients here is so simple in structure that most gins, with their fresh botanical aroma, will work.

Fill the larger half of a cocktail shaker with cubed ice. Add the gin, lemon juice, triple sec and sugar syrup, then seal the shaker and shake. Double strain into the chilled glass, garnish with a lemon twist that's had its oils expressed over the surface of the liquid and serve.

Note: This cocktail is balanced to be more on the sour than sweet side. Try it out as it is, but feel free to add a touch more sugar if it's too sour for you.

GIN

LEMON JUICE

TRIPLE SEC

SUGAR SYRUP

SCOTCH DAISY

50ml (1⅔oz) Scotch whisky

25ml (⅔oz plus 1 tsp) lemon juice

15ml (½oz) triple sec

10ml (2 tsp) Sugar Syrup
(see page 59)

twist of lemon peel or long lemon

Total drink volume: 120ml (4oz)

Ideal glass volume: 150–250ml
(5–8½oz)

Glass: chilled large coupette

Here we keep the structure of a Gin Daisy (see page 155) with the same quantity of spirit, lemon juice, triple sec and sugar, but the flavour profile changes to something warmer, spicier and slightly gentler in sour taste. The grain and wood notes of the Scotch round off the lemon juice, while any peaty notes you may have in your chosen whisky add a touch of smoky length to the flavour of this cocktail.

Fill the larger half of a cocktail shaker with cubed ice. Add the Scotch whisky, lemon juice, triple sec and sugar syrup, then seal the shaker and shake. Double strain into the chilled glass, garnish with twist of lemon peel or long lemon that's had its oils expressed over the surface of the liquid and serve.

Note: If you are a whisky fan, or just curious, experimenting with the type of whisky here will be of interest. You should be able to alter the flavour profile of the cocktail by paying attention to the qualities of the spirit that you select.

SCOTCH WHISKY

LEMON JUICE

TRIPLE SEC

SUGAR SYRUP

AVIATION

50ml (1⅔oz) gin
25ml (⅔oz plus 1 tsp) lemon juice
10ml (2 tsp) Sugar Syrup
  (see page 59)
5ml (1 tsp) maraschino liqueur
maraschino cherry

Total drink volume: 110ml (3⅔oz)
Ideal glass volume: 150–250ml
  (5–8½oz)
Glass: chilled large coupette

Our starting cocktail – the Daisy (see page 155) – is now evolving with a switch to a different fruit: cherry. This is one of my favourite drinks, but then I love cherry. The floral, almost marzipan notes of maraschino sit beautifully against gin, citrus and sour as a taste.

Maraschino liqueur is intense in flavour, so we need less of it to make an impact. You'll notice we've gone from 15ml (½oz) of triple sec in the Daisy to 5ml (1 tsp) of maraschino here. Importantly, we have kept the initial structure of spirit, sour and sweet, meaning we retain a balanced taste while showcasing a new fruit-based flavour profile.

Fill the larger half of a cocktail shaker with cubed ice. Add the gin, lemon juice, sugar syrup and maraschino liqueur, then seal the shaker and shake. Double strain into the chilled glass, garnish with a maraschino cherry and serve.

Note: Historically, violet liqueur was used in an Aviation, which is quite an acquired taste. Switching to maraschino liqueur creates a floral cocktail that better suits a more 'modern-day', universal palate.

GIN

LEMON JUICE

SUGAR SYRUP

MARASCHINO LIQUEUR

DAIQUIRI

50ml (1⅔oz) light rum
25ml (⅔oz plus 1 tsp) lime juice
15ml (½oz) Sugar Syrup
  (see page 59)
twist of lime peel

Total drink volume: 110ml (3⅔oz)
Ideal glass volume: 150–250ml
  (5–8½oz)
Glass: chilled large coupette

Our base recipe of 50ml of spirit, 25ml of sour and 15ml of sweet follows us through into this rum sour cocktail, the Daiquiri. Note the change from lemon to lime juice and the effect. Lime juice is more acidic than lemon juice, and with its resinous note, a little more complex in flavour. However, light rum gives an impression of sweetness and has an almost 'juicy' note to it, so we retain balance even though the acid level has changed. This means we don't need to reduce the volume of lime juice in the cocktail.

Fill the larger half of a cocktail shaker with cubed ice. Add the light rum, lime juice and sugar syrup, then seal the shaker and shake. Double strain into the chilled glass, garnish with a lime twist and serve.

LIGHT RUM

LIME JUICE

SUGAR SYRUP

HEMINGWAY DAIQUIRI

50ml (1²⁄₃oz) light rum

25ml (⅔oz plus 1 tsp) pink
    grapefruit juice

15ml (½oz) lime juice

5ml (1 tsp) maraschino liqueur

5ml (1 tsp) Sugar Syrup
    (see page 59)

lime wheel

Total drink volume: 120ml (4oz)

Ideal glass volume: 150–250ml
    (5–8½oz)

Glass: chilled large coupette

Our friend maraschino is back! Building on a classic Daiquiri (see opposite), the addition of pink grapefruit juice gives, among other things, a slightly woody note that sits well against the cherry-marzipan flavour of the maraschino. This is a fruity, fresh and fun cocktail.

Fill the larger half of a cocktail shaker with cubed ice. Add the light rum, pink grapefruit juice, lime juice, maraschino liqueur and sugar syrup, then seal the shaker and shake. Double strain into the chilled glass, garnish with the lime wheel and serve.

Note: Be conscious of the fact that fresh juices will change in flavour over the seasons. Be aware of the quality of your juices, particularly when it comes to sour and sweet tastes. You may occasionally need to adjust the sugar level in a cocktail.

LIGHT RUM

PINK GRAPEFRUIT JUICE

LIME JUICE

MARASCHINO LIQUEUR

SUGAR SYRUP

From left to right: Daiquiri (see page 160) and Cosmopolitan (see page 164)

COSMOPOLITAN

40ml (1⅓oz) vodka

15ml (½oz) triple sec

20ml (⅔oz) cranberry juice

5ml (1 tsp) lime juice

1.25ml (¼ tsp) Sugar Syrup
   (see page 59)

lime slice

Total drink volume: 100ml (3⅓oz)

Ideal glass volume: 150–250ml
   (5–8½oz)

Glass: chilled large coupette

This iconic modern cocktail goes in and out of fashion, but as it has a vodka base and distinctive sour taste, I wanted to include it in this chapter. I have to admit, this is a hard drink to balance, as its two souring agents – lime and cranberry juice – need a bit of care and attention. Because of this complex sour relationship, our spirit base has dropped in volume. This helps to soften the effect of the acid and keep the drink from being overly intense as a whole experience.

Fill the larger half of a cocktail shaker with cubed ice. Add the vodka, triple sec, cranberry juice, lime juice and sugar syrup, then seal the shaker and shake. Double strain into the chilled glass, garnish with a lime slice and serve.

Note: The type of cranberry juice you use in this cocktail will drastically change the results. I used a high-quality, natural concentrated juice, as I wanted flavour without too much dilution, which is sometimes the problem when working with juices. Test this cocktail before you serve to a guest; your juice may be sweeter, sourer or less intense in flavour and you may need to adjust the recipe slightly by adding more or less cranberry juice. Pay attention to the sugar too; I felt just a touch worked for me, but do increase if your cocktail feels thin in flavour.

VODKA

CRANBERRY JUIEC

LIME JUICE

TRIPLE SEC

SUGAR SYRUP

SIDECAR

50ml (1⅔oz) Cognac

25ml (⅔oz plus 1 tsp) triple sec

25ml (⅔oz plus 1 tsp) lemon juice

5ml (1 tsp) Sugar Syrup
   (see page 59)

sugar rim (see page 39)

Total drink volume: 125ml
   (4oz plus 1 tsp)

Ideal glass volume: 150–250ml
   (5–8½oz)

Glass: large coupette

The Sidecar goes back to 50ml of base spirit for our first step and 25ml of souring agent, lemon juice. But a change in structure comes with a change in volume of the triple sec and sugar. Triple sec is a liqueur, so it has an alcohol content and sweetness. Its function here is to build on the citrus aroma of the lemon, intensifying the overall citrus flavour of the cocktail. This is why it needs to increase in volume, to sit correctly against the Cognac. With that change, we have to reduce the sugar syrup by 5ml or our sour cocktail will be too sweet. We also have a sugar rim to drink from if we need an extra touch of sweetness as we consume. As you might suspect, with these structural changes, this cocktail is a little punchier to drink.

Make a sugar rim on the glass following the instructions on page 39. Fill the larger half of a cocktail shaker with cubed ice. Add the Cognac, triple sec, lemon juice and sugar syrup, then seal the shaker and shake. Double strain into the sugar-rimmed glass and serve.

COGNAC

LEMON JUICE

TRIPLE SEC

SUGAR SYRUP

MARGARITA

50ml (1⅔oz) tequila blanco
25ml (⅔oz plus 1 tsp) triple sec
25ml (⅔oz plus 1 tsp) lime juice
lime wedge
salt rim (see page 39)

Total drink volume: 120ml (4oz)
Ideal glass volume: 150–200ml
(5–6⅔oz)
Glass: rocks glass or large
coupette

Nothing beats a night spent with friends, Mexican food and a Margarita. Triple sec, as you should now expect, builds complexity into the flavour of this cocktail. A note on the salt rim: only apply salt to half the glass. That way your guests can choose how much salt they would like to taste with each sip, making the experience more personalized.

Make a salt rim on half the glass following the instructions on page 39. Fill the larger half of a cocktail shaker with cubed ice. Add the tequila blanco, triple sec and lime juice, then seal the shaker and shake. Double strain into the salt-rimmed glass, garnish with a lime wedge and serve.

Note: Tequila blanco is the classic option for this cocktail's spirit base. If you are a tequila fan, then feel free to experiment with the tequila you use and take note of the effect on the flavour within the structure of this classic cocktail. You will hopefully learn something about the quality and potential of your selected tequila.

TEQUILA BLANCO

TRIPLE SEC

LIME JUICE

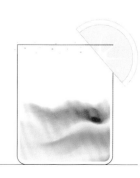

TOMMY'S MARGARITA

50ml (1⅔oz) tequila blanco

25ml (⅔oz plus 1 tsp) Agave Syrup (see page 59)

25ml (⅔oz plus 1 tsp) lime juice

lime wedge

salt rim (see page 39)

Total drink volume: 120ml (4oz)

Ideal glass volume: 150–200ml (5–6⅔oz)

Glass: rocks glass or large coupette

To make a Tommy's Margarita, all we do is swap the triple sec for agave syrup, otherwise the recipe stays the same. The agave gives us a sweetness and warmth along with a little roundness and body in texture and taste.

Make a salt rim on half the glass following the instructions on page 39. Fill the larger half of a cocktail shaker with cubed ice. Add the tequila blanco, agave syrup and lime juice, then seal the shaker and shake. Double strain into the salt-rimmed glass, garnish with a lime wedge and serve.

 TEQUILA BLANCO

 AGAVE SYRUP

 LIME JUICE

MEZCAL MARGARITA

50ml (1⅔oz) mezcal
25ml (⅔oz plus 1 tsp) triple sec
25ml (⅔oz plus 1 tsp) lime juice
lime wedge
salt rim (see page 39)

Total drink volume: 120ml (4oz)
Ideal glass volume: 150–200ml
   (5–6⅔oz)
Glass: rocks glass or
   large coupette

The switch of our base spirit from tequila to mezcal produces a Margarita that is complex in flavour. Here, the resinous, herbal and smoky qualities of the spirit will shine through.

Make a salt rim on half the glass following the instructions on page 39. Fill the larger half of a cocktail shaker with cubed ice. Add the mezcal, triple sec and lime juice, then seal the shaker and shake. Double strain into the salt-rimmed glass, garnish with a lime wedge and serve.

Note: A mezcal and tequila blend will also work well in this cocktail, creating a drink that sits between a traditional Margarita and the mezcal version. Stay within the total volume of 50ml (1⅔oz) of spirit to retain balance, but feel free to try different proportions of mezcal and tequila and see what you think of the flavour result.

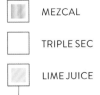

MEZCAL

TRIPLE SEC

LIME JUICE

TOREADOR

50ml (1⅔oz) tequila blanco

25ml (⅔oz plus 1 tsp) apricot
   liqueur

25ml (⅔oz plus 1 tsp) lime juice

lime wedge

Total drink volume: 120ml (4oz)

Ideal glass volume: 150–200ml
   (5–6⅔oz)

Glass: chilled large coupette

Fruit flavours make a welcome return in the last agave-based sour cocktail in this chapter, the Toreador. The warm, stone-fruit juiciness of apricot liqueur sits somewhere between triple sec and agave syrup on the flavour spectrum. So if you happen to have apricot liqueur to hand, it's worth trying this cocktail out and maximizing on the use of this ingredient.

Fill the larger half of a cocktail shaker with cubed ice. Add the tequila blanco, apricot liqueur and lime juice, then seal the shaker and shake. Double strain into the chilled glass, garnish with a lime wedge and serve.

TEQUILA BLANCO

APRICOT LIQUER

LIME JUICE

WHISKEY SOUR

50ml (1⅔oz) Bourbon

25ml (⅔oz plus 1 tsp) lemon juice

25ml (⅔oz plus 1 tsp) egg white

15ml (½oz) Sugar Syrup

   (see page 59)

2 dashes of Angostura bitters,

   plus 1 dash to garnish

Total drink volume: 135ml (4½oz)

Ideal glass volume: 150–200ml

   (5–6⅔oz)

Glass: chilled large coupette or

   rocks glass

The Whiskey Sour, as we discussed in the introduction to this chapter, is our founding structure for sours with foam. This cocktail provides a whole new way to experience whiskey, and in this case Bourbon is the classic go-to. Here, the malty, sweet and rich flavours of Bourbon contrast with the sharper, brighter taste of the lemon juice. The egg white foam rounds the whole experience off through a soft texture. I don't believe you need to be a whiskey drinker to enjoy this cocktail.

Add the Bourbon, lemon juice, egg white, sugar syrup and 2 dashes of Angostura bitters to a cocktail shaker, then seal the shaker and dry shake. Open the shaker and pour the liquid into the smaller half while you fill the larger half with cubed ice. Pour the liquid over the ice. Reseal the shaker and shake. Strain into the chilled glass, garnish with 1 dash of Angostura bitters and serve.

Note: If you can't consume eggs and are looking to use a vegan foaming product, all you need to do is take out the egg white from the recipe and refer to the recommended dosage of your selected foaming product for the best results.

BOURBON

LEMON JUICE

EGG WHITE

SUGAR SYRUP

ANGOSTURA BITTERS

From left to right: New York Sour (see page 174) and Whiskey Sour (see page 171)

NEW YORK SOUR

50ml (1⅔oz) Bourbon

25ml (⅔oz plus 1 tsp) lemon juice

25ml (⅔oz plus 1 tsp) egg white

15ml (½oz) Sugar Syrup
  (see page 59)

15ml (½oz) red wine, to garnish

Total drink volume: 150ml (5oz)

Ideal glass volume: 180–200ml
  (6–6⅔oz)

Glass: chilled large coupette or
  rocks glass

When we move to the New York Sour, the flavour profile of the liquid shifts sideways in a new direction. While red wine on a Whiskey Sour might sound strange, it really does work. The tannins and any oak notes in your red wine will bridge with the Bourbon, while the juicy red grape note that is the body of red wine combines with sweet and sour to produce a delicious fruity effect.

Add the Bourbon, lemon juice, egg white and sugar syrup to a cocktail shaker, then seal the shaker and dry shake. Open the shaker and pour the liquid into the smaller half while you fill the larger half with cubed ice. Pour the liquid over the ice. Reseal the shaker and shake. Strain into the chilled glass, slowly pour the red wine on top of the cocktail for the float garnish and serve.

Note: A red wine with a balanced structure and fruity aroma will suit best here. You can also try using port if you have some to hand.

BOURBON

LEMON JUICE

EGG WHITE

SUGAR SYRUP

RED WINE

SCOTCH WHISKY SOUR

50ml (1⅔oz) Scotch whisky

25ml (⅔oz plus 1 tsp) lemon juice

25ml (⅔oz plus 1 tsp) egg white

15ml (½oz) Sugar Syrup
   (see page 59)

2 dashes of Angostura bitters,
   plus 1 dash to garnish

Total drink volume: 135ml (4½oz)

Ideal glass volume: 150–200ml
   (5–6⅔oz)

Glass: chilled large coupette or
   rocks glass

Like the Daisy (see page 155), the Whiskey Sour has a flexible enough structure that we can play with the spirit base to produce different flavour results in the cocktail. This is a slightly smoky, brighter drink. I find the Scotch dominates a little more in the overall flavour.

Add the Scotch whisky, lemon juice, egg white, sugar syrup and 2 dashes of Angostura bitters to a cocktail shaker, then seal the shaker and dry shake. Open the shaker and pour the liquid into the smaller half while you fill the larger half with cubed ice. Pour the liquid over the ice. Reseal the shaker and shake. Strain into the chilled glass, garnish with 1 dash of Angostura bitters and serve.

Note: If this drink will work with Scotch, it will work with other whiskies. So should you have a selection of whiskies, feel free to experiment and explore their potential.

SCOTCH WHISKY

LEMON JUICE

EGG WHITE

SUGAR SYRUP

ANGOSTURA BITTERS

AMARETTO SOUR

50ml (1⅔oz) Amaretto

25ml (⅔oz plus 1 tsp) lemon juice

25ml (⅔oz plus 1 tsp) egg white

2.5ml (½ tsp) Sugar Syrup
 (see page 59)

Total drink volume: 120ml (4oz)

Ideal glass volume: 150–200ml
 (5–6⅔oz)

Glass: chilled large coupette or
 rocks glass

Amaretto is, on its own, a bit of an indulgent treat. So putting it in a sour turns this golden nutty liquid into a playful, almost kitsch experience. If I don't know what cocktail mood I'm in, an Amaretto Sour is my go-to option, with its non-challenging aromas and balanced sweet and sour taste.

Add the Amaretto, lemon juice, egg white and sugar syrup to a cocktail shaker, then seal the shaker and dry shake. Open the shaker and pour the liquid into the smaller half while you fill the larger half with cubed ice. Pour the liquid over the ice. Reseal the shaker and shake. Strain into the chilled glass and serve.

Note: For a sour cocktail, this drink is on the sweeter side, hence the reduction in sugar syrup in this recipe. Feel free to balance the sugar to your taste.

AMARETTO

LEMON JUICE

EGG WHITE

SUGAR SYRUP

ARMY AND NAVY

50ml (1⅔oz) gin

25ml (⅔oz plus 1 tsp) lemon juice

15ml (½oz) Orgeat (see page 60)

discarded lemon disc

Total drink volume: 110ml (3⅔oz)

Ideal glass volume: 150–200ml
  (5–6⅔oz)

Glass: chilled large coupette

The texture in this recipe doesn't come from a foam like in the other recipes in this section. Orgeat, an almond milk-based syrup, has a fat content as well as a delicious almond flavour. When we shake this syrup in a cocktail, we emulsify it with the other ingredient to create a wonderful silky texture. This cocktail is a serious crowd pleaser – it's approachable and simple, with a delicious flavour.

Fill the larger half of a cocktail shaker with cubed ice. Add the gin, lemon juice and orgeat, then seal the shaker and shake. Double strain into the chilled glass, express the oils from the lemon disc over the surface of the liquid, discard it and serve.

GIN

LEMON JUICE

ORGEAT

WHITE LADY

50ml (1⅔oz) gin

25ml (⅔oz plus 1 tsp) lemon juice

25ml (⅔oz plus 1 tsp) egg white

15ml (½oz) triple sec

10ml (2 tsp) Sugar Syrup
(see page 59)

twist of lemon peel

Total drink volume: 145ml
   (4⅔oz plus 1 tsp)

Ideal glass volume: 150–200ml
   (5–6⅔oz)

Glass: chilled large coupette

This recipe should look familiar to you. If we remove the egg white from it, we are back to our Gin Daisy recipe (see page 155). Here, you can expect the same botanical, citrus and bright flavour of a Daisy, but it is softened by the textural experience a foam brings.

Add the gin, lemon juice, egg white, triple sec and sugar syrup to a cocktail shaker, then seal the shaker and dry shake. Open the shaker and pour the liquid into the smaller half while you fill the larger half with cubed ice. Pour the liquid over the ice. Reseal the shaker and shake. Strain into the chilled glass, garnish with the lemon twist without expressing the oils and serve.

Note: Here we don't express the oils from the lemon, as it would destroy the foam on the top of the drink.

GIN

LEMON JUICE

EGG WHITE

TRIPLE SEC

SUGAR SYRUP

CLOVER CLUB

50ml (1⅔oz) gin

25ml (⅔oz plus 1 tsp) lemon juice

25ml (⅔oz plus 1 tsp) egg white

15ml (½oz) raspberry syrup

15ml (½oz) dry vermouth

Total drink volume: 150ml (5oz)

Ideal glass volume: 180–200ml
  (6–6⅔oz)

Glass: chilled large coupette

My first Clover Club highlighted the potential for flavour within the structure of a cocktail. We still have our founding steps of 50ml of spirit, 25ml of sour, 25ml of texture and 15ml of sweet. We also have a 15ml float of dry vermouth, a highly aromatized liquid more commonly found with gin in a Martini.

Now imagine the flavour profile and experience of a Martini as a 3-D shape, a compressed concertina. Imagine stretching out the Martini concertina. Imagine that each peak and trough is one individual aroma note. The peaks will be the top notes of lemon and orange, coriander seed, juniper, maybe some floral or light herbal notes. The troughs will be the base notes of orris, liquorice, barks and heavier herbal notes. We can move from left to right and start to imagine how our experience of a Martini builds and changes over time.

Through examining this structure, we can start to see the space between each fold, taking note of the shapes that are starting to form here. And we can also start to imagine what other aromas would 'fit' well in that space. Raspberry suddenly looks like a logical fit with gin and dry vermouth. This is what I call the 'space' or 'gaps' between aroma. It's where I like to explore the potential of a cocktail as a vehicle for overall flavour. When I take this point of view, I can understand how this classic cocktail will work, build an expectation of my experience and hopefully be inspired to create something new in the future.

Add the gin, lemon juice, egg white, raspberry syrup and dry vermouth to a cocktail shaker, then seal the shaker and dry shake. Open the shaker and pour the liquid into the smaller half while you fill the larger half with cubed ice. Pour the liquid over the ice. Reseal the shaker and shake. Strain into the chilled glass and serve.

GIN

LEMON JUICE

EGG WHITE

RASPBERRY SYRUP

DRY VERMOUTH

CHAPTER 10:
LONG COCKTAILS

Long cocktails offer us a unique opportunity: we get to explore the potential of a spirit through a higher dilution rate. Apart from a few exceptions (such as the Americano, see page 144, which while being a bitter cocktail is also classed as a long drink), so far most of our cocktails have been powerful and impactful. That's not to say that the flavour of a long cocktail is less of an experience or not valuable – it is actually quite the opposite. Long cocktails give us the opportunity to, in a sense, relax. Their extra dilution, through soda water or a mixer, gives us a lower-ABV experience and that is something to be valued.

The dilution also changes the intensity of the flavour we experience, and while I'm all for flavour making an impact, sometimes we do want an almost 'subconscious' experience. It's a bit like comfort food, and when you don't really know what will satisfy, a long cocktail often does the trick. It becomes a safe place to start, as it's not likely to overwhelm the senses. It's something that as a consumer you don't really have to think about; all you need to do is sit back, relax and enjoy.

And as a host, long cocktails become a great tool to master. If you have guests who are new to drinking cocktails or you're unsure of their personal preferences, a long cocktail is a great solution. These cocktails are also built in the glass they are consumed in, making them quick to make and easy to clean up after, which ultimately buys you time to sit back, relax and have fun.

STRUCTURE CONTINUED...

As you work your way through the cocktails in this chapter, I'm hoping you will notice two things. Firstly, a number of these drinks embrace simplicity. Cocktails such as the Whisky Highball (see page 203) focus on the quality of a spirit and allow its flavour profile to shine through dilution and bubbles.

The second thing you should recognize is the structure of the sour cocktail. A number of the cocktails in this chapter work to the same founding recipe of 50ml of spirit, 25ml of acid and 15ml of sugar. This gives us a core we can rely on while we add additional dilution and, in some cases, flavour. So if sour cocktails are a little too intense for you, do try a Tom Collins (see page 185) and see if this widens your personal preferences.

ADDITIONAL DILUTION

15ML SUGAR SYRUP

25ML ACID

50ML SPIRIT

THE ART OF THE MIXER

I'm very happy to say that bubbles are back! A key part of the attraction of a long cocktail is the fizz; it's the bright, tingling texture that bubbles bring to a liquid that makes this category of cocktails distinctive. Therefore, always make sure your mixers are fresh and still have their fizz, otherwise your long cocktails will be underwhelming.

The trapped CO_2 within mixers will, as it forms bubbles, transport the aromatics held within the body of the liquid to the surface. This aids in our orthonasal perception (see page 70) of the cocktail's aromatic profile, providing us with an enjoyable aromatic experience.

Finally, using a mixer in a cocktail gives us a drink of a larger volume than we have previously seen. This is of benefit to us, as the extra volume comes from an ingredient that contains no alcohol and means we get to enjoy a cocktail that has a lower ABV. Long cocktails therefore become a vital tool in our curation of a cocktail menu – as well as varying the flavour intensity experience, they allow us to offer a balanced selection of ABVs to guests.

INGREDIENTS FOR LONG COCKTAILS

FROM YOUR DRINKS CABINET

Angostura bitters
Bourbon
Cognac
Crème de cassis
Dark rum
Gin
Japanese whisky or an equivalent
Scotch whisky
Light rum
Tequila blanco
Triple sec
Vodka

ADDITIONAL ITEMS

Fresh lemons
Fresh limes
Fresh mint
Fresh pink grapefruits
Ginger ale
Ginger beer
Pickled gherkins or cornichons
Sea salt flakes
Soda water
Spiced tomato juice
Sugar Syrup (see page 59)
Tabasco sauce
Worcestershire sauce

TOM COLLINS

50ml (1⅔oz) gin

25ml (⅔oz plus 1 tsp) lemon juice

15ml (½oz) Sugar Syrup
   (see page 59)

100ml (3⅓oz) soda water

lemon wheel

cubed ice, to serve

Total drink volume: 190ml (6⅓oz)

Ideal glass volume: 300ml (10oz)

Glass: highball

This recipe should look familiar, as we move back to the founding structure of spirit, sweet and sour we established in the sour cocktails chapter (see page 151). The relationship of these three ingredients, plus the addition of soda water, produces a cocktail that is incredibly refreshing.

Fill the glass with ice, add the gin, lemon juice and sugar syrup and stir 3 times to combine. Check the level of ice in the glass – if necessary, add more to ensure it reaches the top of the glass. Top up the drink with the soda water, gently stir 3 times to combine, garnish with a lemon wheel and serve.

Note: Pick your favourite gin for this cocktail and pay attention to how its aroma opens up in the soda water.

GIN

LEMON JUICE

SUGAR SYRUP

SODA WATER

TRIPLE SEC COLLINS

40ml (1⅓oz) triple sec

25ml (⅔oz plus 1 tsp) lemon juice

5ml (1 tsp) Sugar Syrup
(see page 59)

100ml (3⅓oz) soda water

lemon slice

cubed ice, to serve

Total drink volume: 170ml (5⅔oz)
Ideal glass volume: 300ml (10oz)
Glass: highball

Swapping the gin for triple sec produces an almost sherbet-like Collins cocktail. Note that the recipe change is driven by the sugar content of the triple sec, as well as the intensity of its citrus aroma. Bubbles help us here, as their texture on the palate changes how we perceive the sweetness in this liqueur.

Fill the glass with ice, add the triple sec, lemon juice and sugar syrup and stir 3 times to combine. Check the level of ice in the glass – if necessary, add more to ensure it reaches the top of the glass. Top up the drink with the soda water, gently stir 3 times to combine, garnish with a lemon slice and serve.

Note: Try this cocktail with any crème liqueur you have to hand, but do test the recipe before you serve it to guests. Be aware of the cocktail's overall balance and intensity of flavour if you switch to a different liqueur.

TRIPLE SEC

LEMON JUICE

SUGAR SYRUP

SODA WATER

CASSIS COLLINS

40ml (1⅓oz) crème de cassis

25ml (⅔oz plus 1 tsp) lemon juice

100ml (3⅓oz) soda water

lemon slice

cubed ice, to serve

Total drink volume: 165ml (5½oz)
Ideal glass volume: 300ml (10oz)
Glass: highball

The fruity blackcurrant notes that make up a big part of the flavour profile of crème de cassis can be fully appreciated in this Collins twist. As with the Triple Sec Collins recipe (see opposite), the sugar in the founding structure of this cocktail has been reviewed in order to create a balanced drink that is not overly sweet. Therefore, there is no additional sugar in this Collins.

Fill the glass with ice, add the crème de cassis and lemon juice and stir 3 times to combine. Check the level of ice in the glass – if necessary, add more to ensure it reaches the top of the glass. Top up the drink with the soda water, gently stir 3 times to combine, garnish with a lemon slice and serve.

 CRÈME DE CASSIS

 LEMON JUICE

SODA WATER

GIN RICKY

50ml (1⅔oz) gin

25ml (⅔oz plus 1 tsp) lime juice

15ml (½oz) Sugar Syrup
   (see page 59)

100ml (3⅓oz) soda water

twist of lime peel

cubed ice, to serve

Total drink volume: 190ml (6⅓oz)

Ideal glass volume: 300ml (10oz)

Glass: highball

Here we move back to the relationship created with 50ml of spirit, 25ml of acid and 15ml of sugar, but a simple swap from lemon to lime provides a whole new flavour profile and turns a Tom Collins (see page 185) into a Gin Ricky. When tasting this drink, note the difference in acidity and aromatics that comes with a switch to lime juice. The cocktail should feel less sweet and drier in taste when compared with lemon; you might also detect a pine-like aroma from the lime that the gin will amplify.

Fill the glass with ice, add the gin, lime juice and sugar syrup and stir 3 times to combine. Check the level of ice in the glass – if necessary, add more to ensure it reaches the top of the glass. Top up the drink with the soda water, gently stir 3 times to combine, garnish with a lime twist and serve.

Note: A green botanical gin will work very well in this cocktail. You can also try the exact same recipe with vodka to produce a delicious result.

GIN

LIME JUICE

SUGAR SYRUP

SODA WATER

BOURBON RICKY

50ml (1⅔oz) Bourbon

25ml (⅔oz plus 1 tsp) lime juice

15ml (½oz) Sugar Syrup
   (see page 59)

100ml (3⅓oz) soda water

twist of lime peel

cubed ice, to serve

Total drink volume: 190ml (6⅓oz)

Ideal glass volume: 300ml (10oz)

Glass: highball

Sticking with lime juice and the flavour it brings, we now switch the spirit used in this Ricky cocktail and examine how this changes the drink's flavour profile. We still have a dry acid note from the lime juice, but a complexity in aroma of candied fruit peels and malt has been added via the Bourbon. This makes for an interesting cocktail which perhaps tastes fresher than expected.

Fill the glass with ice, add the Bourbon, lime juice and sugar syrup and stir 3 times to combine. Check the level of ice in the glass – if necessary, add more to ensure it reaches the top of the glass. Top up the drink with the soda water, gently stir 3 times to combine, garnish with a lime twist and serve.

Note: A fruity, lighter Bourbon such as Maker's Mark works well in this cocktail.

BOURBON

LIME JUICE

SUGAR SYRUP

SODA WATER

MOJITO

leaves from 2 sprigs of mint

25ml (⅔oz plus 1 tsp) lime juice

15ml (½oz) Sugar Syrup
  (see page 59)

50ml (1⅔oz) light rum

75ml (2⅓oz plus 1 tsp) soda water

mint sprig

lime wheel

cubed ice, to serve

Total drink volume: 165ml (5½oz)

Ideal glass volume: 300ml (10oz)

Glass: highball

Along with a shift in spirit base in our founding structure, we now explore the addition of a herb to create a new cocktail experience in this category of drinks. The Mojito is iconic; its bright green aroma placed against a fresh, juicy light rum creates a cocktail that signifies summertime and fun.

Add the mint leaves, lime juice and sugar syrup to a cocktail tin. Using a muddler, gently break the skin of the leaves so that they release their oils into the liquid. Fill the glass with ice and add the light rum, then double strain the mint-muddled liquid into the glass and stir 3 times to combine. Check the level of ice in the glass – if necessary, add more to ensure it reaches the top of the glass. Top up the drink with the soda water, gently stir 3 times to combine, garnish with a mint sprig and lime wheel and serve.

LIGHT RUM

LIME JUICE

SUGAR SYRUP

SODA WATER

MOSCOW MULE

50ml (1⅔oz) vodka

15ml (½oz) lime juice

3 dashes of Angostura bitters

100ml (3⅓oz) ginger beer

lime wedge

cubed ice, to serve

Total drink volume: approximately 165ml (5½oz)

Ideal glass volume: 300ml (10oz)

Glass: highball

Mixers can add a great deal of flavour to a cocktail and this is where our focus shifts slightly. This is the first cocktail in this category to use a flavoured mixer, in this case ginger beer. Our relationship of spirit to acid is retained, but as ginger beer contains sugar, we no longer need any additional sugar in the cocktail. We stick with the green flavour of lime, use a cleaner base spirit of vodka and add complexity and depth through the addition of Angostura bitters, which bridge the gap between the spiciness of the ginger beer, the vodka and the lime. The result is an overall clean and precise spiced flavour.

Fill the glass with ice, add the vodka, lime juice and Angostura bitters and stir 3 times to combine. Check the level of ice in the glass – if necessary, add more to ensure it reaches the top of the glass. Top up the drink with the ginger beer, gently stir 3 times to combine, garnish with a lime wedge and serve.

 VODKA

LIME JUICE

ANGOSTURA BITTERS

GINGER BEER

From left to right: Mojito (see page 190) and Moscow Mule (see page 191)

DARK AND STORMY

50ml (1⅔oz) dark rum
15ml (½oz) lime juice
100ml (3⅓oz) ginger beer
3 dashes of Angostura bitters
lime wedge
cubed ice, to serve

Total drink volume: approximately 165ml (5½oz)
Ideal glass volume: 300ml (10oz)
Glass: highball or rocks glass

Ginger continues to be our focus and takes the lead as we add the profiles of dark rum, lime and Angostura. The spiced molasses profile of dark rum creates a rich and warming cocktail.

Fill the glass with ice, add the dark rum and lime juice and stir 3 times to combine. Check the level of ice in the glass – if necessary, add more to ensure it reaches the top of the glass. Top up the drink with the ginger beer and gently stir 3 times to combine. Garnish with 3 dashes of Angostura bitters, which will initially float on top of the liquid and create a marbled effect. Add a lime wedge and serve.

Note: Adding the bitters at the end produces a visually stunning result. However, there is a consequence to this – we perceive the Angostura bitters quite intensely at the start of sipping this drink. If this is not to your taste, consider stirring the drink before sipping or add the bitters to the glass at the same time as you add the dark rum and lime juice.

 DARK RUM

 LIME JUICE

 ANGOSTURA BITTERS

 GINGER BEER

WHISKEY HORSE'S NECK

50ml (1⅔oz) Bourbon

3 dashes of Angostura bitters

100ml (3⅓oz) ginger ale

extra-long lemon peel

regular cubed ice or 1 long chunk,
   to serve

Total drink volume: approximately
   150ml (5oz)

Ideal glass volume: 300ml (10oz)

Glass: highball

The Horse's Neck has no acid element in the drink, but builds complexity through ginger ale and Angostura bitters. Ginger ale is softer in flavour than ginger beer, which is useful here, as the lack of acid in this cocktail means there is less of a founding structure for a powerful aroma like ginger to sit neatly against. Intensity of flavour is leading our ingredient choice here.

Fill the glass with ice cubes or a long chunk of ice, add the Bourbon and Angostura bitters and stir 3 times to combine. If using regular cubed ice, check the level of ice in the glass – if necessary, add more to ensure it reaches the top of the glass. Top up the drink with the ginger ale and gently stir 3 times to combine. Garnish with an extra-long lemon peel coiled around the ice inside the glass and serve.

Note: Rye whiskey can be use here and will produce a drier-tasting cocktail. Feel free to increase or decrease the volume of bitters depending upon how aromatic you'd like this cocktail to taste.

■ BOURBON

■ ANGOSTURA BITTERS

□ GINGER ALE

COGNAC HORSE'S NECK

50ml (1⅔oz) Cognac, such as
Merlet Brothers Blend VSOP
3 dashes of Angostura bitters
100ml (3⅓oz) ginger ale
extra-long lemon peel
regular cubed ice or 1 long chunk,
to serve

Total drink volume: approximately
150ml (5oz)
Ideal glass volume: 300ml (10oz)
Glass: highball

This Cognac variation produces a cocktail that is perhaps a little more subtle than its Bourbon counterpart. I've used Merlet Brothers Blend in this cocktail, as I find its white fruit and gentle oak notes produce a drink that is incredibly smooth and moreish.

Fill the glass with ice cubes or a long chunk of ice, add the Cognac and Angostura bitters and stir 3 times to combine. If using regular cubed ice, check the level of ice in the glass – if necessary, add more to ensure it reaches the top of the glass. Top up the drink with the ginger ale and gently stir 3 times to combine. Garnish with an extra-long lemon peel coiled around the ice inside the glass and serve.

 COGNAC

 ANGOSTURA BITTERS

GINGER ALE

From left to right: Paloma (see page 200) and Whiskey Horse's Neck (see page 196)

PALOMA

50ml (1⅔oz) tequila blanco
50ml (1⅔oz) pink grapefruit juice
15ml (½oz) lime juice
15ml (½oz) Sugar Syrup
   (see page 59)
75ml (2⅓oz plus 1 tsp) soda water
lime wedge
regular cubed ice or 1 long chunk,
   to serve
salt rim (see page 39)

Total drink volume: 205ml
   (6⅔oz plus 1 tsp)
Ideal glass volume: 300ml (10oz)
Glass: highball or rocks glass

This bright citrus-led long cocktail is a great alternative to a Margarita (see page 166), especially if you want a sour agave-based cocktail that doesn't involve shaking. The addition of 15ml (½oz) of lime juice adds a little complexity and depth to the sour taste and overall flavour of this drink.

Make a salt rim on the glass following the instructions on page 39. Fill the glass with ice cubes or a long chunk of ice, add the tequila blanco, pink grapefruit juice, lime juice and sugar syrup and stir 3 times to combine. If using regular cubed ice, check the level of ice in the glass – if necessary, add more to ensure it reaches the top of the glass. Top up the drink with the soda water and gently stir 3 times to combine. Garnish with the lime wedge and serve.

Note: There is a lot going on in this cocktail, so it is robust enough to stand up to and work with mezcal. Do try this if you have mezcal to hand, as the smoky notes will perfectly complement the slightly woody citrus aroma of pink grapefruit.

TEQUILA BLANCO

PINK GRAPEFRUIT JUICE

LIME JUICE

SUGAR SYRUP

SODA WATER

EL DIABLO

50ml (1⅔oz) tequila blanco
25ml (⅔oz plus 1 tsp) lime juice
15ml (½oz) crème de cassis
100ml (3⅓oz) ginger beer
lime wedge
cubed ice, to serve

Total drink volume: 190ml (6⅓oz)
Ideal glass volume: 300ml (10oz)
Glass: highball

Ginger beer has a powerful flavour that we can use to our advantage; it gives us a very robust structure to work with and balance against. The juicy agave note that the tequila brings, matched with the warm fruity blackcurrant notes of crème de cassis, makes this cocktail a mouth-watering experience.

Fill the glass with ice, add the tequila blanco, lime juice and crème de cassis and stir 3 times to combine. Check the level of ice in the glass – if necessary, add more to ensure it reaches the top of the glass. Top up the drink with the ginger beer, gently stir 3 times to combine, garnish with a lime wedge and serve.

Note: There is room for experimentation with this cocktail via a switch in liqueur. Take your lead from the tequila and ginger beer and explore what other fruity flavours complement them.

 TEQUILA BLANCO

LIME JUICE

CRÈME DE CASSIS

GINGER BEER

WHISKY HIGHBALL

25ml (⅔oz plus 1 tsp) Japanese
   whisky
1.25ml (¼ tsp) Sugar Syrup
   (see page 59)
75ml (2½oz plus 1 tsp) soda water
regular cubed ice or 1 large cube,
   to serve

Total drink volume:
   approximately 100ml (3½oz)
Ideal glass volume: 150ml (5oz)
Glass: highball

This cocktail has gained in popularity in recent years; its light and approachable flavour makes it a great aperitif cocktail to serve before dinner. It is also one of the simplest of the long highball cocktails: we allow the whisky to take centre stage and be appreciated through dilution and bubbles, providing a moment of clarity and simplicity.

The Whisky Highball has a long heritage in Japan, with products such as Suntory Whisky Toki designed to work perfectly in this cocktail. The green, fresh and light aromas of this style of whisky make this drink very approachable from a flavour point of view, but a light Scotch whisky will also work well.

Fill the glass with ice, add the whisky and sugar syrup and stir 3 times to combine. If using regular cubed ice, check the level of ice in the glass – if necessary, add more to ensure it reaches the top of the glass. Top up the drink with the soda water, gently stir 3 times to combine and serve.

Note: I like to use a small Japanese highball glass, as I feel it presents the perfect volume of liquid for an aperitif drink. A 25ml (⅔oz plus 1 tsp) spirit serve is therefore appropriate, but if you are working with a larger glass, do scale the recipe up.

A number of great Japanese drinking vinegars are now available from online suppliers – a small dash can add a touch of life to a drink. If you are looking to explore the potential of the Whisky Highball, try adding 1.25–2.5ml (¼–½ tsp) of one of these aromatic, sweet-and-sour balanced vinegars to the cocktail and see what you think.

JAPANESE WHISKY

SUGAR SYRUP

SODA WATER

BLOODY MARY

50ml (1⅔oz) vodka

15ml (½oz) Worcestershire sauce

15ml (½oz) pickle juice
  from the jar

5ml (1 tsp) Tabasco sauce

100ml (3⅓oz) spiced tomato juice

small pickled gherkin or
  cornichon

half a long lemon peel

cubed ice, to serve

Total drink volume: 185ml
  (6oz plus 1 tsp)
Ideal glass volume: 300ml (10oz)
Glass: highball

An iconic umami-rich cocktail, the Bloody Mary is perfect for brunch, lunch or early-evening occasions. The quality of tomato juice will make the biggest impact on the structure of this cocktail, so get the best that you can find and one that suits your taste preference. Pay attention to how the Worcestershire sauce and pickle juice sit against the structure of your selected tomato juice – if it leans towards the sweet or sour tastes, you may need to increase or decrease the volume of these two ingredients.

Fill the glass with ice, add the vodka, Worcestershire sauce, pickle juice and Tabasco and stir 3 times to combine. Check the level of ice in the glass – if necessary, add more to ensure it reaches the top of the glass. Top up the drink with the spiced tomato juice and gently stir 3 times to combine. Garnish with a small pickle and half a long lemon peel and serve.

Note: A Bloody Mary is a personal thing and you may like more or less spice in yours, so adjust the dosage of the Tabasco sauce if you wish. If you don't have pickles and therefore pickle juice, substitute this ingredient with fresh lemon juice. If you only have large pickles, cut one in half lengthways to suit the size of your glass. You can also take out the vodka to make a great-tasting Virgin Bloody Mary.

VODKA

WORCESTERSHIRE SAUCE

PICKLE JUICE

TABASCO SAUCE

SPICED TOMATO JUICE

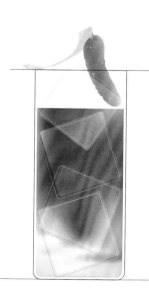

CHAPTER 11:
EVOLVING YOUR
DRINKS AT HOME

At the start of this book, we set out on a path of discovery to explore how cocktails work and deliver a flavour experience. Along the way we've learned about the methods used to make them, the ingredients, the structure of mixed liquids and our personal tastes. My aim was to help you make cocktails at home in a logical and efficient way. I hope that by learning these lessons, cocktails now seem more approachable to you. This chapter, in a sense, presents 'hacks', as we try to solve the problem of missing cocktail ingredients and start a bespoke flavour exploration. Ultimately, I hope that through the confidence you have built, you'll feel inspired to try new flavours, experiment and continue on your journey exploring flavour in a liquid format.

NOW WE UNDERSTAND STRUCTURE...

For a moment, I'd like to revisit how we approach cocktail making and highlight a few of the key principles we raised at the start of our journey. We established that structure is the arrangement and relationship between a cocktail's ingredients, and that our goal is balance. The sensation of alcohol and the basic tastes of sweet, sour, bitter and in some cases salt and umami should all be in pleasing proportion to each other. Remember, we are not saying that these tastes should all be equally as strong as each other, but that they should together create a whole new taste experience. Aroma and texture are added to the mix to complete the overall flavour structure of the cocktail.

We now know how to pay attention to the effect of the flavour of our ingredients – one change will affect how the other ingredients in the recipe work together. As our approach, at all times, is based on this awareness, we can start to explore making changes to a cocktail, whether it's because we prefer different flavours or because we have a cocktail emergency and are missing an ingredient in the original recipe. With any type of problem solving, it's important to start with what you know. Therefore, the recipes in this chapter are rooted in structures we have already visited. You should spot the familiarities and understand the logic in the evolution of the ingredients.

THE LOGIC AND EFFICIENCY OF SUBSTITUTIONS

We can only be efficient when we have the capability to look at what we have to hand and use it wisely. This is why versatile products make up the backbone of a good cocktail cabinet; one bottle of balanced gin opens the door to a vast number of drinks. Whether the drinks are stirred, bitter or sour, this gin will work, so is an efficient product to use. But what if we take this approach and look at some of the ingredients we have to hand in the kitchen? Suddenly we have the potential to be efficient with non-traditional cocktail ingredients, which is useful as well as fun.

By understanding a cocktail's structure, we can understand the functionality of its ingredients. We know which ingredients are adding a taste such as sweet or sour, which ingredients are providing an aroma and what the profile of that aroma is. These are our building block, and being able to identify what we have in front of us means we can look to the wider world of ingredients and flavour to explore how a cocktail might be rebuilt, if necessary, in a slightly different way. So when it comes to ingredient substitutions, our first question is: what is the key functionality of the ingredient we are trying to replace? This will guide us on where to start to look in our kitchen for substitutions. For example, the key function of lemon juice in a Tom Collins (see page 185) is acid. What other ingredients do I have that add acid to food? I might look at my selection of vinegars as a starting point. My next question is, how intense in taste is lemon juice and how intense are the other ingredients in a Tom Collins? This will inform me on which acid I need to select. In this case I would need something gentle. As the other ingredients are gin, sugar and soda, the aromatic profile of this cocktail is light and aromatic, and my acid choice must complement that. Malt vinegar and white wine vinegar would each have a very different effect.

With this thought process there will ultimately be a lot of trial and error. Some things you try just won't work or you won't like them. Don't be disheartened – with every change you try, keep your mind open and pay attention to what you experience so that you learn something. I often learn most from the mistakes I make and find it much easier to identify why I don't like something than why I do. Accept the fact that although they need to taste balanced and pleasing, these cocktails will never taste exactly the same as their original. But that's something we can live with if needs must. And you have now opened yourself up to my world – you are now a cocktail recipe developer! Let the following key points guide you:

1   Keep it simple. Focus on one change at a time so that you can understand the full effect of that change. Often, less is more.

2   Think about the basic tastes and ABV you may need to replace. Make sure these are balanced correctly in the new ingredient you use.

3   Look at the aromatic profile of the ingredient you need to imitate. What do you have to hand that runs parallel with this profile? Keeping it simple and identifying key drivers such as fruity, green or floral will guide you.

4   Write down any variations you try and like. Trust me, you'll be grateful next time.

WISE HOSTING

Hosting should be enjoyable, but sometimes it is stressful. Keeping guests happy, with a drink in hand, is a skill that mainly comes down to timing. If you are wise with your cocktail choices for the occasion, prepped and set up correctly, you'll find that you've saved yourself time on making and cleaning up. The pay-off here is more time to have fun with your guests. The final part of this book presents a selection of cocktails that, in advance of the occasion, can be batched in larger quantities and stored ready for use. Which means more time for you to enjoy hosting.

When it comes to batching cocktails, there are a few practical considerations to take into account. I've summarized these points below so that you can easily refer back when making batched cocktails.

- As we won't be stirring or shaking these batched liquids with ice, we risk serving cocktails that are at a slightly warmer temperature than is normal. As you should now know, this is an issue, as a warmer temperature changes how we perceive the intensity of sweetness and ABV. Therefore, it's important that batched liquids are made at least a few hours in advance and left in the fridge to chill down fully before serving.
- Building on the above point, cold glassware will really help you to reach the ideal serving temperature for batched liquids. Don't overlook this – consider chilling your glasses.
- I like to store batched liquids in sealed bottles in the fridge and ensure there is as little air as possible in the bottle. Just like with wine, this helps to slow down any oxidation of the liquid. You can reuse empty spirit bottles to do this. When it comes to serving your drinks, you can always transfer the liquid to a more appropriate carafe or jug if you prefer.
- I've noted a shelf life for each recipe, as there is a risk with batched cocktails that you will have some left over at the end of the occasion. This shelf life is a recommendation only. Some batched liquids will keep for longer and still taste good, but be aware their flavours will change over time, possibly dulling down and seeming less fresh.

JAM KIR ROYALE

15ml (½oz) Jam Liqueur
(see below)
115ml (3⅔oz plus 1 tsp)
Champagne

Total drink volume: 130ml (4⅓oz)
Ideal glass volume: 165–285ml
(5½–9½oz)
Glass: Champagne flute or tulip at
room temperature

As it has one of the most simple structures, the Kir Royale was the first cocktail recipe we explored together (see page 82). As a cocktail, its flavour goal is to present Champagne with the addition of a rich and warm fruity flavour that is neither too sweet nor too acidic. Taking this goal into account, there is no reason why we can't look at what a liqueur is and make our own with what we have to hand. The key thing to think about here is the balance of the liqueur. Vodka is one of the most useful ingredients we can work with, as its neutral flavour provides us with a spirit base we can push in any direction we wish.

Note that the recipe for jam liqueur below contains water, as we want to lower the ABV of the vodka to something more suitable and closer to that of crème de cassis. I used raspberry jam when trying this recipe, but any jam should work. I recommend you first make a small batch of cocktails with your selected jam to test that the intensity and balance of flavour is correct. Feel free to add more or less jam if needed.

Add the jam liqueur to the glass and top up with the Champagne. Using a bar spoon, gently stir the liquid to combine, then serve.

Jam liqueur: Add 50ml (1⅔oz) each of vodka, water and jam to a jug and stir until the jam has dissolved. Pass the mixture through a fine sieve to remove any fruit bits or seeds. Retain the strained liquid for use. Makes 130ml (4⅓oz).

JAM LIQUEUR (vodka, water, jam)

CHAMPAGNE

HONEY KIR ROYALE

**15ml (½oz) Honey Liqueur
(see below)**
**115ml (3⅔oz plus 1 tsp)
Champagne**

Total drink volume: 130ml (4⅓oz)
Ideal glass volume: 165–285ml
(5½–9½oz)
Glass: Champagne flute or tulip at
room temperature

Champagne is very enjoyable on its own, but sometimes a mood or occasion leads to the desire for a simple twist. Here, we look at the function of aroma in a liqueur and how this sits against Champagne. Honey, with its warm nutty, floral aroma, is a perfect match. There are so many varieties of honey available, each with their own distinct aroma profile, so we have an interesting ingredient to experiment with.

If you compare the honey liqueur recipe below with the jam liqueur recipe on page 210, you'll notice that we have a larger proportion of honey to liquid. This decision is driven by the intensity in flavour of the honey – we need a little more, as it is more delicate, not acidic and less sweet than jam.

Add the honey liqueur to the glass and top up with the Champagne. Using a bar spoon, gently stir the liquid to combine, then serve.

Honey liqueur: Add 25ml (⅔oz plus 1 tsp) each of vodka and water to a jug with 50ml (1⅔oz) of your selected honey and stir until the honey has dissolved. Retain the liquid for use. Makes 100ml (3⅓oz).

HONEY LIQUEUR (vodka, water, honey)

CHAMPAGNE

TEA 'MARTINI'

50ml (1⅔oz) gin
5ml (1 tsp) Cold-brewed Early
Sparrow Green Tea (see below)
5ml (1 tsp) Cold-brewed Hadong
Black Tea (see below)
5ml (1 tsp) verjus
green olive or disc of lemon peel

Total drink volume: approximately
85ml (2⅔oz plus 1 tsp)
Ideal glass volume: 100–150ml
(3⅓–5oz)
Glass: chilled coupette

My goal with this adapted drink was to create a stirred cocktail that resembled the dry, palate-cleansing properties of a Dry Gin Martini (see page 104), but that used no dry vermouth. Once opened, dry vermouth tends to oxidize, even if kept in the fridge. It can go off without you realizing it, which is an issue if you spontaneously decide to make a Martini. Although this cocktail is not really a Martini, it offers a clean, focused and dry drinking experience that runs parallel to a Dry Martini.

Here, a cold water extraction of high-quality green and black teas provides the most refined and complex structure to work with. These particular teas are somewhat specialist, so feel free to use what you have to hand and focus on creating a balanced structure of tannins and aromatics for your cocktail.

Fill a cocktail tin with cubed ice. Add the gin, cold-brewed teas and verjus and stir approximately 15 times to combine. Double strain into your chilled glass, garnish with an olive (for a more savoury experience) or lemon disc that's had its oils expressed over the surface of the liquid (for a more aromatic experience) and serve.

Cold-brewed tea: Combine 100ml (3⅓oz) of cold filtered water and 2.5g (1 tsp) of tea leaves in a jug. Stir gently so that the tea is submerged. Cover and leave to infuse at room temperature for 1 hour. When ready, strain the liquid through a coffee filter and retain for use. Makes 75ml (2⅓oz plus 1 tsp).

GIN

COLD-BREWED EARLY SPARROW GREEN TEA

COLD-BREWED HADONG BLACK TEA

VERJUS

CLASSIC ESPRESSO MARTINI

50ml (1⅔oz) vodka

25ml (⅔oz plus 1 tsp) coffee
liqueur

25ml (⅔oz plus 1 tsp) freshly
made espresso

5ml (1 tsp) Sugar Syrup
(see page 59)

Total drink volume: approximately
120ml (4oz)

Ideal glass volume: 150ml (5oz)

Glass: chilled coupette

When I was thinking about cocktails to adapt, the Espresso Martini was high on my list to explore. If you have an espresso machine, whether it's a classical set-up or pod-based system, follow the recipe below for a Classic Espresso Martini. If you don't, follow the recipe opposite for a (No) Espresso Martini – it requires a little more preparation, but still results in a cocktail with a strong coffee kick. The key is to use a high-quality and robust ground coffee.

Fill the larger half of a cocktail shaker with cubed ice. Add the vodka, coffee liqueur, espresso and sugar syrup, then seal the shaker and shake. Double strain into the chilled glass and serve.

Note: I find coffee liqueurs quite sweet, but I've added a small amount of sugar syrup to this recipe, as it balances against the bitterness of the coffee and provides added texture. This may be something you'd like to reduce or increase depending on your personal taste.

VODKA

COFFEE LIQUER

FRESHLY MADE ESPRESSO

SUGAR SYRUP

(NO) ESPRESSO MARTINI

50ml (1⅔oz) **Coffee-infused**
Vodka (see below)

25ml (⅔oz plus 1 tsp) **coffee**
liqueur

25ml (⅔oz plus 1 tsp) **Brewed**
Coffee (see below)

10ml (2 tsp) **Sugar Syrup**
(see page 59)

Total drink volume: approximately
120ml (4oz)

Ideal glass volume: 150ml (5oz)

Glass: chilled coupette or
chilled espresso cups

Fill the larger half of a cocktail shaker with cubed ice. Add the coffee-infused vodka, coffee liqueur, brewed coffee and sugar syrup, then seal the shaker and shake. Double strain into the chilled glass or cup and serve.

Note: If hosting, you can pre-batch this recipe before your guests arrive and store the liquid in a bottle in the fridge. When it comes to serving, shake the liquid according to the instructions in the recipe. I like to serve this to guests as an after-dinner digestive cocktail in espresso cups.

Coffee-infused vodka: Combine 400ml (13½oz) of rye vodka and 60g (2oz) of ground coffee in a jug. Stir gently so that the coffee is submerged. Cover and leave to infuse at room temperature for 30 minutes. When ready, strain the liquid through a coffee filter and retain for use. Makes 300ml (10oz).

Brewed coffee: Combine 350ml (11⅔oz) freshly boiled water and 60g (2oz) of ground coffee in a jug. Stir gently so that the coffee is submerged. Cover and leave to infuse at room temperature for 30 minutes. When ready, strain the liquid through a coffee filter and retain for use. Makes 250ml (8½oz).

 COFFEE INFUSED VODKA

COFFEE LIQUER

BREWED COFFEE

SUGAR SYRUP

(No) Espresso Martini (see page 215)

STORE CUPBOARD WHISKEY SOUR

50ml (1⅔oz) Bourbon

25ml (⅔oz plus 1 tsp) lemon juice

15ml (½oz) Sugar Syrup
(see page 59)

⅓ dropper of Ms. Better's Bitters
Miraculous Foamer

2 dashes of Angostura bitters,
plus 1 dash to garnish

Total drink volume: approximately
125ml (4oz plus 1 tsp)

Ideal glass volume: 150–200ml
(5–6⅔oz)

Glass: chilled large coupette or
rocks glass

There are some clever products available on the market designed as long-shelf-life substitutions for short-shelf-life products, such as egg whites. These products are also useful if you need to accommodate dietary requirements – in this case, always check the label of your selected substitution to ensure it is suitable for your needs.

Add the Bourbon, lemon juice, sugar syrup, Ms. Better's Bitters Miraculous Foamer and 2 dashes of Angostura bitters to a cocktail shaker, then seal the shaker and dry shake. Open the shaker and pour the liquid into the smaller half while you fill the larger half with cubed ice. Pour the liquid over the ice. Reseal the shaker and shake. Strain into the chilled glass, garnish with 1 dash of Angostura bitters and serve.

BOURBON

LEMON JUICE

SUGAR SYRUP

MS BETTER'S MIRACULOUS FOAMER

ANGOSTURA BITTERS

STORE CUPBOARD HIGHBALL

50ml (1⅔oz) gin

25ml (⅔oz plus 1 tsp) verjus

15ml (½oz) Sugar Syrup
   (see page 59)

100ml (3⅓oz) soda water

fresh herb sprig or fruit

cubed ice, to serve

Total drink volume: 190ml (6⅓oz)

Ideal glass volume: 300ml (10oz)

Glass: highball

Here we use the structure of a Tom Collins (see page 185) but with a long-shelf-life product to replace one of our key structural ingredients, the lemon juice. So if you are short on lemons and spontaneously decide to make a Tom Collins-style cocktail, you are not limited by the lack of a fresh ingredient. When it comes to a garnish, feel free to be playful. If you have any fresh herbs or fruit to hand that you feel would work, try it out.

Fill the glass with ice, add the gin, verjus and sugar syrup and stir 3 times to combine. Check the level of ice in the glass – if necessary, add more to ensure it reaches the top of the glass. Top up the drink with the soda water and gently stir 3 times to combine. Garnish with a selected herb sprig or fruit and serve.

GIN

VERJUS

SUGAR SYRUP

SODA WATER

BATCHED GIMLET

500ml (17oz) gin
250ml (8½oz) lime cordial
200ml (6⅔oz) filtered water
10 discs of lime peel

Batch volume: 950ml (32oz)
Individual serves: 10
Total drink volume: 95ml
  (3oz plus 1 tsp)
Ideal glass volume: 100–150ml
  (3⅓–5oz)
Glass: chilled coupette
Batch shelf life: 48 hours

This simple recipe is a great one to consider batching, as its flavour profile is so balanced that it suits most guests' tastes. You may like to change the flavour of cordial you use – this is a great way to link your cocktail to any food you may be serving, so consider taking that into account.

Add the gin, lime cordial and filtered water to a suitably sized jug and stir to combine. Keep in the jug or decant into a bottle and store in the fridge to chill down. When serving, pour the chilled liquid straight into a chilled glass and garnish with a lime disc that's had its oils expressed over the surface of the liquid.

GIN

LIME CORDIAL

FILTERED WATER

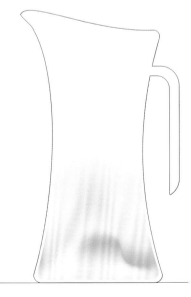

BATCHED SWEET MANHATTAN

400ml (13½oz) Bourbon

200ml (6⅔oz) sweet vermouth

25ml (⅔oz plus 1 tsp) maraschino liqueur

11 dashes of Angostura bitters

200ml (6⅔oz) filtered water

11 maraschino cherries

Batch volume: 825ml (27⅔oz)

Individual serves: 11

Total drink volume: approximately 75ml (2⅓oz plus 1 tsp)

Ideal glass volume: 100–150ml (3⅓–5oz)

Glass: chilled coupette

Batch shelf life: 1 week

Stirred cocktails are perfect for batching. They tend to be spirit-focused with few fresh ingredients, so they will be very stable when batched and stored in a fridge. A Sweet Manhattan (see page 117) is my choice here – it's classy and guests appreciate the slightly fruity flavour. Feel free to pick your favourite stirred cocktail and see what you can batch.

Add the Bourbon, sweet vermouth, maraschino liqueur, Angostura bitters and filtered water to a suitably sized jug and stir to combine. Keep in the jug or decant into a bottle and store in the fridge to chill down. When serving, pour the chilled liquid straight into a chilled glass and garnish with a maraschino cherry.

BOURBON

SWEET VERMOUTH

MARASCHINO LIQUER

ANGOSTURA BITTERS

FILTERED WATER

BATCHED MARGARITAS

500ml (17oz) tequila blanco
250ml (8½oz) triple sec
250ml (8½oz) lime juice
200ml (6⅔oz) filtered water
10 lime wedges
cubed ice, to serve
salt rims (see page 39)

Shaken drinks aren't normally made in advance. The process of shaking adds texture to the cocktail and we miss out on this if we make them in advance. However, I'm a firm believer that Margaritas (see page 166) are just what's required for a group of friends and a table full of Mexican food, so I'm going to bend the rules and give you a batched Margarita recipe. I like to add ice to the finished cocktails here – the drink can take the extra dilution and benefits from the drop in temperature ice brings.

Batch volume: 1.2 litres (40oz)
Individual serves: 10
Total drink volume: 120ml (4oz)
Ideal glass volume: 150–200ml (5–6⅔oz)
Glass: rocks glass
Batch shelf life: 24 hours

Add the tequila blanco, triple sec, lime juice and filtered water to a suitably sized jug and stir to combine. Keep in the jug or decant into a bottle and store in the fridge to chill down. Make a salt rim on half of each glass following the instructions on page 39. When serving, pour the chilled liquid straight into the salt-rimmed glasses that have been filled with cubed ice.

TEQUILA BLANCO

TRIPLE SEC

LIME JUICE

FILTERED WATER

A DRINK FOR EVERY OCCASION

A SWEET MOMENT

A SAVOURY MOMENT

A DRY MOMENT

AN AROMATIC MOMENT

APERITIVO HOUR

BEFORE DINNER

AFTER DINNER

INDEX OF DRINKS BY KEY SPIRIT

ABSINTHE

DEATH IN THE
AFTERNOON,
page 84

SAZERAC RYE,
page 131

SAZERAC
COGNAC,
page 132

AGAVE SPIRITS

MEZCAL

SMOKY ROYALE,
page 88

MEZCAL OLD
FASHIONED,
page 130

MEZCAL
NEGRONI,
page 142

MEZCAL
MARGARITA,
page 169

TEQUILA

TEQUILA OLD
FASHIONED,
page 129

MEZCAL OLD
FASHIONED,
page 130

MARGARITA,
page 166

TOMMY'S
MARGARITA,
page 168

TOREADOR,
page 170

PALOMA,
page 200

EL DIABLO,
page 201

COGNAC

CHAMPAGNE
COCKTAIL,
page 90

FRENCH 75,
page 95

HARVARD,
page 121

SAZERAC
COGNAC,
page 132

SIDECAR,
page 165

COGNAC
HORSE'S NECK,
page 197

GIN

FRENCH 75,
page 95

DRY GIN
MARTINI,
page 104

WET GIN
MARTINI,
page 106

DIRTY GIN
MARTINI,
page 107

GIBSON,
page 108

MARTINEZ,
page 115

NEGRONI,
page 140

GIMLET,
page 109

GIN DAISY,
page 155

AVIATION,
page 158

ARMY AND
NAVY, page 177

WHITE LADY,
page 178

CLOVER CLUB,
page 181

TOM COLLINS,
page 185

GIN RICKY,
page 188

TEA 'MARTINI',
page 213

STORE
CUPBOARD
HIGHBALL,
page 219

RUM

LIGHT RUM

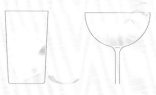

AIRMAIL,
page 96

DAIQUIRI,
page 160

HEMINGWAY
DAIQUIRI,
page 161

MOJITO,
page 190

GOLDEN RUM

RUM SWEET
MANHATTAN,
page 119

EL PRESIDENTE,
page 123

RUM OLD
FASHIONED,
page 126

DARK RUM

DARK AND
STORMY,
page 195

VODKA

TWINKLE,
page 89

VODKA MARTINI,
page 112

DIRTY VODKA
MARTINI,
page 113

SHERRY
MARTINI,
page 114

VODKA OLD
FASHIONED,
page 127

COSMOPOLITAN,
page 164

MOSCOW MULE,
page 191

BLOODY MARY,
page 204

CLASSIC
ESPRESSO
MARTINI,
page 214

(NO)
ESPRESSO
MARTINI,
page 215

WHISKY

BOURBON

SWEET MANHATTAN, page 117

PERFECT MANHATTAN, page 118

OLD FASHIONED, page 124

BOULEVARDIER, page 143

WHISKEY SOUR, page 171

NEW YORK SOUR, page 174

BOURBON RICKY, page 189

WHISKEY HORSE'S NECK, page 196

STORE CUPBOARD WHISKEY SOUR, page 218

SCOTCH WHISKY

ROB ROY, page 120

SCOTCH OLD FASHIONED, page 125

SCOTCH DAISY, page 156

SCOTCH WHISKY SOUR, page 175

RYE WHISKY

SAZERAC RYE, page 131

JAPANESE WHISKY

WHISKY HIGHBALL, page 203

LIQUEURS

AMARETTO

AMARETTO SOUR,
page 176

APRICOT LIQUEUR

SMOKY ROYALE,   TOREADOR,
page 88   page 170

CAMPARI

MILANO   NEGRONI,   MEZCAL   BOULEVARDIER,   AMERICANO,   SPAGLIATO,
TORINO,   page 140   NEGRONI,   page 143   page 144   page 146
page 139   page 142

COFFEE LIQUEUR

CLASSIC ESPRESSO
MARTINI, page 214

CRÈME DE CASSIS

KIR ROYALE,   CASSIS COLLINS,   EL DIABLO,
page 82   page 187   page 201

MARASCHINO LIQUEUR

MARTINEZ,
page 115

SWEET
MANHATTAN,
page 117

RUM SWEET
MANHATTAN,
page 119

ROB ROY,
page 120

AVIATION,
page 158

HEMINGWAY
DAIQUIRI,
page 161

TRIPLE SEC

EL PRESIDENTE,
page 123

GIN DAISY,
page 155

SCOTCH DAISY,
page 156

COSMOPOLITAN,
page 164

SIDECAR,
page 165

MARGARITA,
page 166

MEZCAL
MARGARITA,
page 169

WHITE LADY,
page 178

TRIPLE SEC
COLLINS,
page 186

WINES

CHAMPAGNE

KIR ROYALE,
page 82

DEATH IN THE
AFTERNOON,
page 84

BLACK VELVET,
page 85

SMOKY ROYALE,
page 88

TWINKLE,
page 89

CHAMPAGNE
COCKTAIL,
page 90

SHERRY
CHAMPAGNE
COCKTAIL,
page 92

MIMOSA,
page 93

FRENCH 75,
page 95

AIRMAIL,
page 96

JAM KIR ROYALE,
page 210

HONEY KIR
ROYALE,
page 212

PROSECCO

SPAGLIATO,
page 146

SPRITZ,
page 149

RED WINE

NEW YORK SOUR,
page 174

SHERRY

SHERRY
CHAMPAGNE
COCKTAIL,
page 92

SHERRY MARTINI,
page 114

VERMOUTH

DRY VERMOUTH

DRY GIN MARTINI, page 104

WET GIN MARTINI, page 106

DIRTY GIN MARTINI, page 107

GIBSON, page 108

VODKA MARTINI, page 112

DIRTY VODKA MARTINI, page 113

PERFECT MANHATTAN, page 118

CLOVER CLUB, page 181

SWEET VERMOUTH

MARTINEZ, page 115

SWEET MANHATTAN, page 117

PERFECT MANHATTAN, page 118

RUM SWEET MANHATTAN, page 119

ROB ROY, page 120

HARVARD, page 121

EL PRESIDENTE, page 123

MILANO TORINO, page 139

NEGRONI, page 140

MEZCAL NEGRONI, page 142

BOULEVARDIER, page 143

AMERICANO, page 144

SPAGLIATO, page 146

INDEX

Page numbers in **bold** indicate cocktail recipes.

AUTHOR'S ACKNOWLEDGEMENTS

Thank you to LSA, Richard Brendon, Malfatti Glass and Ichendorf Milano for crafting the wonderful glassware that was used throughout this book.

To Holly and the team at Octopus, your faith and drive with the project has been amazing and so appreciated.

Andre, Luis and Lola; you are my photography dream team! I can't wait until the next time.

Ashley, Angus and Becca – shaken cocktails will never be the same again; these recipes are especially for you!

A special thanks to Belen Aloisi – I will always value your logical and precise questions and the moments of celebration you instigated. And to my friend 'The Brain' – I know in the most lovely of ways you can't lie, so your feedback meant more than most to me.

ABOUT THE AUTHOR

ZOE BURGESS studied at Chelsea College of Art and worked in the artisanal chocolate sector before specializing in drinks development.

She is one of the UK's most renowned flavour experts and founding partner of one of east London's most unique and creative cocktail bars, Untitled.

With a career spanning over 10 years in the drinks industry, she developed groundbreaking cocktail menus for giants of the hospitality industry such as Pernod Ricard and internationally renowned Michelin-starred chef Heston Blumenthal. Zoe has collaborated with some of the world's most respected sensory scientists, including Oxford University's Charles Spence and the University of London's pioneering chemist Andrea Sella.

In 2019, Zoe founded her own independent flavour consultancy, Atelier Pip. One of her key passions is pushing the boundaries within the sensory- and flavour-led sectors to help improve consumers' drinking experience. She continues to work with Heston Blumenthal's creative team as well as new clients such as The Standard Hotel London, Kricket Soho, and Be-oom tea rooms.

www.atelier-pip.com
[Instagram] @atelier_pip

Photo: Lucy Pope